JUST CLIMATE FUTURES

Integrating Social Inclusion Into the Net Zero Transition

Carolyn Snell and Lucie Middlemiss

First published in Great Britain in 2025 by

Bristol University Press
University of Bristol
1–9 Old Park Hill
Bristol
BS2 8BB
UK
t: +44 (0)117 374 6645
e: bup-info@bristol.ac.uk

Details of international sales and distribution partners are available at bristoluniversitypress.co.uk

© Bristol University Press 2025

British Library Cataloguing in Publication Data
A catalogue record for this book is available from the British Library

ISBN 978-1-5292-3987-4 hardcover
ISBN 978-1-5292-3988-1 paperback
ISBN 978-1-5292-3989-8 ePub
ISBN 978-1-5292-3990-4 ePdf

The rights of Carolyn Snell and Lucie Middlemiss to be identified as authors of this work have been asserted by them in accordance with the Copyright, Designs and Patents Act 1988.

All rights reserved: no part of this publication may be reproduced, stored in a retrieval system, or transmitted in any form or by any means, electronic, mechanical, photocopying, recording, or otherwise without the prior permission of Bristol University Press.

Every reasonable effort has been made to obtain permission to reproduce copyrighted material. If, however, anyone knows of an oversight, please contact the publisher.

The statements and opinions contained within this publication are solely those of the authors and not of the University of Bristol or Bristol University Press. The University of Bristol and Bristol University Press disclaim responsibility for any injury to persons or property resulting from any material published in this publication.

Bristol University Press works to counter discrimination on grounds of gender, race, disability, age and sexuality.

Cover design: Liam Roberts Design
Front cover image: Stocksy/Marc Tran

For
Dave, Macy and Max
Derek, George and Ralph

Contents

List of Figures, Tables and Boxes		vi
Notes on Contributors		viii
Acknowledgements		xi
Preface		xii
1	Introduction	1
	Carolyn Snell, Lucie Middlemiss, Emily Morrison and Anne Owen	
2	Net Zero Policy and Climate Futures	19
	Carolyn Snell, Lucie Middlemiss, Kelli Kennedy, Tania Carregha and Anne Owen	
3	A Just Transition?	39
	Carolyn Snell, Lucie Middlemiss, Kelli Kennedy, Tania Carregha, Anne Owen and Samanthi Theminimulle	
4	Rooting Net Zero in Social Thinking	72
	Lucie Middlemiss, Carolyn Snell and Yekaterina Chzhen	
5	Pathway to a Just Climate Future	91
	Lucie Middlemiss, Carolyn Snell, Emily Morrison and Anne Owen	
Notes		111
References		112
Index		138

List of Figures, Tables and Boxes

Figures

1.1	Equivalized two-adult household carbon footprints	13
2.1	Daily interactions with Net Zero policies	20
3.1	Share of total environmental impact covered by 'where we live' by equivalized income decile	41
3.2	Share of total environmental impact covered by 'where we go' by equivalized income decile	48
3.3	Share of total environmental impact covered by 'what we eat' by equivalized income decile	54
3.4	Share of total environmental impact covered by 'what we do for fun' by equivalized income decile	57
3.5	Share of total environmental impact covered by 'spending power' by equivalized income decile	62

Tables

1.1	Overview of the threats to human life created by climate change	16
2.1	Key changes associated with the Net Zero transition	21
2.2	Where we live: examples of relevant policies	23
2.3	Where we go: examples of relevant policies	26
2.4	What we eat: examples of relevant policies	28
2.5	What we do for fun: examples of relevant policies	31
2.6	What we buy: examples of relevant policies	33
2.7	Work life: examples of relevant policies	35
3.1	Existing and potential inequalities under Net Zero – summarized	40
5.1	Key steps towards a just climate future: in summary	99

Boxes

1.1	Visions of a Net Zero society	6
1.2	The causes of anthropogenic climate change	15

3.1	Where we live: the lived experience perspective	40
3.2	Where we go: the lived experience perspective	46
3.3	What we eat: the lived experience perspective	53
3.4	What we do for fun: the lived experience perspective	56
3.5	What we buy: the lived experience perspective	60
3.6	What we do for work: the lived experience perspective	65
4.1	Jim's story: the risks of transition	89
5.1	Understanding how Net Zero will affect your community	100
5.2	Disaggregating data to identify at risk populations	101
5.3	Jim's just climate future	107

Notes on Contributors

While Carolyn Snell and Lucie Middlemiss have led the majority of the writing in this particular publication, the research and thinking that underpins this research has been a collective, collaborative process, with colleagues providing input at different parts of the research and writing process.

The role of the Institute for Community Studies (powered by The Young Foundation) is notable here, given its leadership in the original scope and purpose of the research, and development and implementation of the empirical phases of the research. The role of Emily Morrison in developing the original proposal calling for a systematic analysis of how communities and places will experience and play a vital role in Net Zero, and her research leadership of the project is notable here. Individual inputs have been recognized throughout, with each chapter indicating different colleagues' contributions.

Contributor biographies

Tania Carregha is Senior Research Manager at the Institute for Community Studies, powered by The Young Foundation, with a background in social psychology and design for social innovation. Tania's research focuses on the social implications of environmental policy, social justice and public participation in the transition to Net Zero. Together with Samanthi Theminimulle, she led on the design and delivery of the participatory workshops described in this book, with a focus on accessibility and enabling meaningful participation.

Yekaterina Chzhen is Assistant Professor in the Department of Sociology at Trinity College Dublin. She is a Fellow of Trinity College Dublin and a member of the Trinity Research in Childhood Centre. Her research focuses on inequalities in material wellbeing, education and health across the life course. Prior to joining Trinity College Dublin, she held research positions at the UNICEF Office of Research in Florence and at the University of Oxford.

Kelli Kennedy is Research Associate in Health Sciences at the University of York, as part of the Bradford Health Determinants Research Collaboration working with Bradford Council. Previously she held a post as a researcher to the project this book is based on, contributing to a policy review and various aspects of fieldwork. Her research focuses on health and social policy issues, including around the commercial determinants of health, household food insecurity, and a just transition to Net Zero. Kelli is also a founding member of the Social Policy Association's Climate Justice network.

Lucie Middlemiss is Professor of Environment and Society at the Sustainability Research Institute at the School of Earth and Environment, University of Leeds, where she has worked for 20 years. As a sociologist working on environmental issues, she researches the ways in which people are able to engage in environmental agendas, as well as how lives are shaped by social conditions in conjunction with environmental policy. She is a co-leader of the Leeds Relational Energy Group, and is actively engaged in efforts to bring together practitioners, policy-makers and academics, through her leadership in the Leeds-based Fair Energy Futures network, and the national Fuel Poverty Evidence network.

Emily Morrison is Director of Sustainability and Just Transition at The Young Foundation, Impact Director for the ESRC national JUST Centre, and previously the lead for the Institute for Community Studies, powered by The Young Foundation. Her expertise is in designing, leading and brokering partnerships, tools and impact frameworks to drive social, environmental and place-based impact. Emily leads large scale policy, research and engagement projects that evidence and take action on the social justice and place dimensions of environmental policy, advocating for a just transition to Net Zero. These have included the bilateral US–UK Climate Challenge Cup for Innovation at COP26, the introduction of the Welsh Government's Environmental Governance Bill, and development of multiple local authority and sector strategies to ensure a just transition in the UK. Outside of The Young Foundation, Emily is currently funded by the Leverhulme Trust to examine the implications of long term social and political instability on citizen organization, local environmentalism and social action.

Anne Owen is Associate Professor at the Sustainability Research Institute in the School of Earth and Environment, University of Leeds. Her research focuses on the environmental impacts associated with households and how we can mitigate these. She is particularly interested in how household carbon footprints vary by household type and over time. Anne calculates the UK's carbon footprint for the UK Government and this has now been badged as an Official Statistic and is released annually.

Carolyn Snell is Professor of Social Policy at the School for Business and Society, University of York. Prior to this she held a research post at the Stockholm Environment Institute where she worked on the social and public policy aspects of environmental policies. Her research and publications largely focus on energy policy in the UK, with a particular interest in the intersection of fuel poverty, energy policy, and climate policy. Carolyn is one of the founding members of the Social Policy Association's Climate Justice network.

Samanthi Theminimulle is Senior Researcher at the Institute for Community Studies, powered by The Young Foundation, with an academic background in sociology, degrowth and political ecology. Samanthi's research focuses on place-sensitive policy for a just transition to Net Zero. Together with Tania Carregha, she led on the design and delivery of the participatory workshops described in this book, with a focus on accessibility and enabling meaningful participation.

Acknowledgements

The research underpinning this book was supported by the Nuffield Foundation, under the project title *Understanding Family and Community Vulnerabilities in Transition to Net Zero*. Without which, this work could not have gone ahead.

The authors would like to express their gratitude to the participants from the seven communities in Leeds and Newcastle, who generously shared their time and insights. We also wish to thank Lucie Morin for her assistance with fieldwork activities during her visit to the University of Leeds, and Nancy Levine for her contributions during her Ecology and Conservation Level 3 programme.

Our thanks extend to the members of our Advisory Group: Alex Beer, Patrick Gould, Liz O'Driscoll, Jane Wills, Andrew Richmond, David Craine, Helen Stockton, Elizabeth Blakelock, Jane Robinson, Jonathan Bradshaw, Amelie Trepass and Harriet Thomson.

Additionally, we appreciate the contributions of the following team members, whose support was instrumental in shaping and advancing the research: Gill Main, Richard Harries, Jess Moore, Alice Lemkes and Helen Goulden.

Preface

On 28 June 2021 a group of us representing The Young Foundation, Trinity College Dublin, the University of Leeds, and the University of York had confirmation from the Nuffield Foundation that we had received funding to undertake a project that would seek to 'Understand Family and Community Vulnerabilities in the transition to Net Zero'. The project proposed to explore how disadvantaged people and communities might be affected by the UK's Net Zero policy agenda, and to consider how risks might be mitigated, and communities included and empowered during this period of change.

By the midway point of the project we had produced a 60,000 word report that explored the likely policy changes that were expected to occur over the next 30 years, existing inequalities within these broad areas of policy change, for example fuel poverty and housing, and what had already been written on these areas of policy change from a climate justice perspective – for example changes to home energy systems as a result of low carbon policies and their impacts on different households. Drawing this material together and reflecting on theoretical work around capabilities and social inclusion, our research led to the development of a framework that outlined the challenges that exist for households, and the actions that might be taken to enable a transition to Net Zero that leaves no one behind.

Once we had completed our report, we realized what we had done – rather than reviewing existing literature, we had actually brought together material that had simply not existed in the same place before. Indeed, no one to date had tried to consider the impact of Net Zero-related policies on people as a whole. Even *within* policy areas, the cumulative impact of policy change has rarely been discussed or acknowledged. Moreover, policy changes are often discussed in a technical way, that doesn't recognize difference or different people's existing circumstances. We rectify these gaps in knowledge in our book.

Our book represents a departure from existing work on climate justice and Net Zero, placing people's everyday lives and experiences at its heart. In the later chapters of the book, we draw on theoretical work from the field of social policy, often neglected within environmental social science, to help us understand what inclusion within the transition to Net Zero might look like and entail. Our approach allows us to consider the potential impact of the Net Zero agenda on people as a whole, and the ways in which people may be excluded from participating in it. We end on a positive, transformative note, concluding by outlining the actions that can be taken to ensure an inclusive and just climate future.

Carolyn Snell and Lucie Middlemiss
January 2025

1

Introduction

Carolyn Snell, Lucie Middlemiss, Emily Morrison and Anne Owen

Introduction

> Cost of living and everything has hit us all at the same time. So if you were already struggling … if you're already thinking how am I going to feed and heat … my kids, I'm not then replacing anything unless it comes from the charity shop
>
> Quotation 289, Neighbourhood A, Leeds

> I just worry about this current crisis we've got and whether they … are prepared to invest more because it will cost even more to make all of this happen … Unless they are willing to offer people who can't afford to put in a new heat pump or whatever, then (Net Zero) it's not going to happen.
>
> Quotation 96, Neighbourhood B, Leeds

The Young Foundation's 2019 mass participatory community research exercise documented people's response to the climate crisis, and the associated body of climate policy – commonly known as 'Net Zero', and defined in detail further on – identifying this as the most polarizing issue for the public in the UK (Institute for Community Studies, 2020). Research participants reported that the climate crisis lacked a 'local narrative' about impacts, strategies for adaptation and mitigation, that the time horizons for addressing climate change were long, making it difficult to prioritize, that science-based targets and policies were opaque, uncertain or lacked strong political commitment, and that political U-turns were too frequent. People also asked how they could relate to the challenges of decarbonizing homes, lives, jobs and lifestyles, when issues of poverty, chronic and long-term health conditions, a social care crisis, and economic precarity associated with austerity and Brexit were at the forefront of their minds. This response was in the context of public awareness shifting substantially in the last 5 years: since 2022, the year of the 40°C heat wave in the UK, climate change has consistently ranked in the top five issues that the UK public is most concerned about (Kings College London, 2024).

This leaves us with a conundrum. On the one hand, people care deeply about climate change and want to see leadership and action from government on climate change. On the other, there are important concerns about both governance of climate change, and the difficulties that people are facing in their everyday lives, which make climate policy and action seem overwhelmingly challenging. In effect, people cannot see how just climate futures can be brought about from their present circumstances. These concerns about the feasibility of climate change governance and policy, growing out of the lived experience, are legitimate and important. They are reflective of what we see as the true challenge of reaching Net Zero goals: action to decarbonize our society requires participation of the public, including their acceptance of the need for change, and their involvement in finding and delivering solutions. Given where we find ourselves in 2025 in the UK: recovering from the shock of COVID-19, facing unpredictable weather events, in the wake of a long programme of austerity, this is a big ask. It is made even bigger by the fact that inclusion of the poorest people, households and communities is not a current priority of climate mitigation measures.

In this book we propose a new approach to climate policy, putting people and communities at the heart of reaching Net Zero, which we believe offers the opportunity to resolve this conundrum. We build on the existing evidence base, to show how the transition to low carbon living carries a high risk of reinforcing exclusion and disadvantage. We document how the poorest households and most marginalized communities have been left out of a largely technological transition to date, and face higher risks associated with Net Zero policy in both the short and long term. Our new approach provides the foundational thinking for an emerging emphasis in research, policy and action, which amounts to a recognition of the need to approach the Net Zero transition as a just social transformation. By centring people and places, with due respect for their present experiences and conditions, by identifying the households and communities most at risk of exclusion, and by designing progressive policy and action for maximum social inclusion, we believe that Net Zero could represent an opportunity for a better world. On the other hand, if Net Zero continues as a predominantly environmentally oriented agenda, there is a significant risk of entrenching inequalities, engendering political discontent and, as a consequence, failing to meet our climate goals in any case.

The transition to Net Zero will entail a substantial social transformation. The scale of policy change anticipated here is huge, reaching into much of people's everyday lives. As a result, the UK Government (2022) foresees mixed outcomes, including the risks of unaffordability of mitigation measures and likely job losses in high carbon and declining industries; alongside potential for benefits in green jobs and skills, anticipated lower home running costs, opportunities for local prosperity, new community assets and infrastructures, and the potential for a rise in civic and social engagement. There is substantial evidence of the opportunities for co-benefits of a Net Zero transition: reduced precarity in the cost of living, transformation of long-term employment prospects, and resolution of health harms and health inequities (Jennings et al, 2019; Marmot and Allen, 2020). There is also the potential to capitalize on the shift to a low-carbon future: building a more preventative, cost-effective state, and reducing spatial inequalities for left behind places (APPG for Left Behind Neighbourhoods, 2021). Given the scale of change, however, history tells us that Net Zero is highly likely to result in unfair social, economic, health and place-based outcomes, and decreased societal cohesion, if we do not make *just* climate futures our goal.

Our approach in this book is rooted in an understanding that the places in which we spend our everyday lives, our homes and local communities, are the places in which a low-carbon society will be negotiated and produced. As DEFRA's review of public engagement found, responding to climate change has 'causes and consequences that are translocal (connecting people in many places, and/or across time), with associated costs and benefits unevenly distributed' (DEFRA, 2022: 30). It is hugely important to establish how every household can participate in this agenda, and a critical step towards this is to address the distribution of costs and benefits as they currently stand. This involves more than just economic redistribution, because of the multifaceted nature of social exclusion which we introduce and elaborate in this book. Indeed, how we accept, adopt and sustain low-carbon ways of life is determined by our relationships, economic and social dependencies, culture, social background and historic experiences; and by the choices we have access to, which are in turn mediated by the places we live, the networks and communities we are part of, and who we trust. People and their everyday lives, and places, with their distinctive social and physical infrastructure, must be at the heart of the Net Zero transition.

This book marks the first attempt to bring together the literatures charting the transition scenarios for Net Zero, with a wide range of evidence and data concerning household and community inequality, vulnerability and impacts. We use this enormous body of evidence to show how the experience of a transition to Net Zero will be very different in diverse households, shaped by current inequalities and vulnerabilities but also by the effects of new policy. By drawing in previously neglected thinking from social policy, we are able to more fully articulate social needs for inclusion in Net Zero, and in doing so offer a guide to policymakers and practitioners to build pathways towards truly just climate futures. In the remainder of this chapter, we outline some of the key concepts, concerns and approaches that lie at the heart of this book. We briefly consider climate change as a policy problem, what Net Zero life is likely to look like, consider the concept of the 'just transition', discuss existing gaps in thinking about and making Net Zero policies, and present an introduction to our approach to addressing these issues.

What is Net Zero and the just transition?

Climate change has been described by the UN as 'the defining issue of our time' (UNFCCC, 2023), and as a 'highly complex, intractable, global policy problem' (Gough, 2011) with severe, pervasive and irreversible impacts (Stern, 2007: 23). Recognition that a global response is necessary has grown since the 1980s, with the creation of the Intergovernmental Panel on Climate Change (IPCC) in 1988, the 1997 Kyoto Protocol that set out the world's first GHG reduction strategy, and the 2015 Paris Agreement (see Snell in Yeates and Holden, 2022).

At all levels, policy approaches largely fall into three main categories: loss and damage, adaptation and mitigation (IPCC, 2018; UNEP, 2024). Loss and damage is the most recent policy innovation, aiming to provide financial support to countries adversely affected by climate change (UNEP, 2024). As suggested by its name, adaptation policy approaches attempt to adapt the economy, infrastructure, and society to the climate change itself. Mitigation policies on the other hand, aim to modify climate change, through the reduction of greenhouse gas emissions. The Paris Agreement brought into common use terminology relating to the 'transition to Net Zero' (also expressed as 'low carbon economy', and 'carbon neutrality'). Following the 2015 Paris Agreement, UN Secretary General Antonio Guterres urged a declaration of climate emergencies in all countries until carbon neutrality was accomplished globally (UN, 2024a).

Net Zero and the low carbon economy

The embodiment of climate change mitigation, 'Net Zero' refers to achieving an overall balance between the amount of greenhouse gas produced and the amount removed from the atmosphere. This target reflects the understanding that 'net emissions of CO_2 by human activities ... must approach zero in order to stabilize global mean temperature' (Davis et al, 2018: 1). As discussed throughout this book, action towards Net Zero is multifaceted and wide ranging – including changes within (for example) industry, transport, infrastructure, and agriculture, through to changes that are orchestrated on a very personal level – such as a switch to a low carbon diet. Note that in this book we use the term 'Net Zero' principally as a shorthand for the body of policy aimed at achieving a transition to Net Zero. We also occasionally use it (as in the following sentence) to refer to the target associated with carbon mitigation.

Under the Paris Agreement, Net Zero should be achieved globally by 2050, with the aim of reducing emissions by 45 per cent by 2030. Signatories to the Agreement (the UK included) are committed to reducing their carbon emissions, with emphasis placed on the responsibility of wealthy countries in the global North to reduce emissions the most and fastest. As a result, the vast majority of these countries have committed to achieving Net Zero by 2050, and most have interim targets that are close to or mirror those laid out in the Paris Agreement.

The Paris Agreement was the first to require all countries to create national mitigation plans through Nationally Determined Contributions (NDCs), rather than requiring developed nations to act first, something that underpinned early global climate policy (McGinn and Isenhour, 2021). Given the need for all countries to reduce their emissions, Net Zero strategies, and indeed the language of Net Zero and carbon neutrality have become a common part of the climate policy landscape at the global, international, supranational (the EU has a significant role within climate policy), national and local levels. While the context varies hugely for these policies, at their heart, they require widespread changes to the way societies currently operate, and how they operate in the future.

In 2018 the IPCC starkly set out the extent to which societal transformation for a successful transition to Net Zero is needed. This is within the context of the rapid pace at which greenhouse emissions by nations must peak and decline and carbon outputs be reduced. As such, urgent and rapid action is necessary, requiring the right policies, infrastructures and technologies and institutional and business cooperation (IPCC, 2022) to enable ordinary people to make these changes. It is in this anticipated context of essential but rapid societal change in the coming 25 years that our book is written.

Future visions of life under Net Zero

Visions of life under Net Zero have been produced by policy, grassroots and academic actors. In the UK these have been developed most notably by: The Department for Business, Energy, and Industrial Strategy/Department for Energy Security and Net Zero (BEIS/DESNZ), The Centre for Research into Energy Demand Solutions, The Climate Assembly UK and the UK's Climate Change Committee. These visions are largely consistent in their evocation of a Net Zero world: foreseeing changes across many aspects of everyday life, over a relatively short but shifting time period. From the household or community perspective, this is likely to be experienced as an enormous, challenging and transformative endeavour. Examples relating to mobility, homes, and food are presented in Box 1.1 (and discussed in depth in Chapters 2 and 4). While these summarize Net Zero visions for the UK, they are very similar to other countries within the global North (see for example the exploration of different countries' Net Zero policies by the OECD (2023)).

Box 1.1: Visions of a Net Zero society

Mobility of the future

By 2035 new cars and vans with an internal combustion engine (ICE) will be phased out across most of Europe (with hybrids also phased out by 2035) and replaced with electric vehicles (EVs) or hydrogen vehicles. These changes will affect transport systems as a whole, from private cars, motorbikes and vans, through to HGVs, trains and buses. Alongside the shift to greener vehicles, we expect to see an improvement of active travel and public transport, including the increased use of e-scooters. Cycle lanes and walking routes will also be improved, and made safer and more desirable. Investment in transport infrastructure will become Net Zero focused, with strategic investment in roads requiring justification along these lines. Furthermore, investment in roads will support the roll out of EV charging infrastructure (Climate Change Committee, 2020b).

Homes of the future

A significant change is the move towards greater electricity use within the home. In terms of heating, we are likely to see a shift to the use of heat pumps, increased use of electric systems, and heat networks. Homes are likely to be 'smarter' with heating and lighting controls that enable greater energy efficiency. New builds will be highly energy efficient, and older housing will need to be extensively retrofitted to ensure energy efficiency. Householders will be more tech-savvy and more aware of the need to reduce energy use, and will take positive actions to do this. Engagement with energy providers and services will look very different, for example, those connected to heating networks may experience greater interactions with local government and community-based organizations rather than national energy providers.

Eating in the future

Different visions of Net Zero paint a range of possible future diets: ranging from many more people adopting plant-based diets (veganism), to swapping red meat for white meat or fish, or dairy for legumes. One of the scenarios anticipates people eating more seasonally and locally or having location-appropriate diets (Kim et al, 2020). Other changes likely to be encouraged in the food sector include reducing food waste (along the whole supply chain), reduction of emissions in the farming sector, and reduction of emissions in the food and drink processing sector.

The just transition to Net Zero

Existing research on climate mitigation policy warns that changes that fail to consider existing inequalities risk exacerbating these, harming some of the most vulnerable in society (Gillard et al, 2017; Hasegawa et al, 2018; Robinson and Shine, 2018; Ivanova and Middlemiss, 2021). This is not a new concern within environmental policy where there has been substantial discussion about the need to balance social, economic and environmental objectives (Brundtland, 2005). Justice concerns are commonly raised within climate policy discourse, as policy intended to drive the transition to Net Zero comes with many potential risks, and trade-offs, especially if a solely environmental agenda that fails to consider social needs is pursued.

Transformation towards Net Zero will lead to inevitable trade-offs between social, economic and environmental objectives, with evidence suggesting that these are difficult to meet concurrently (Hussein et al, 2013; Gillard et al, 2017; Hasegawa et al, 2018; Robinson and Shine, 2018). As a result, substantial concerns have been raised about the potential for the transition to Net Zero to disproportionately impact those already experiencing disadvantages (Caplan, 2017; Snell et al, 2022; Kennedy and Snell, 2023), and the risk of pushing households already struggling with poverty, precarity and availability of work and decent income, the cost of living – and other fundamental forms of participation in society – further into deprivation, exclusion, destitution and crisis.

These concerns are increasingly framed in terms of a 'just transition' to Net Zero – drawing on terminology originating from a US trade union movement in the 1970s where concerns were raised about the need to protect jobs while making environmental policy (Wang and Lo, 2021). Substantial concerns have been raised about the potential for the transition to Net Zero to disproportionately impact those already experiencing disadvantages (IPPR, 2018; UNFCCC, 2018; UNRISD and ULIP, 2018). The concept of a just transition is used to draw attention to and articulate such risks. As such, a just transition recognizes the importance of balancing environmental, economic and social objectives to ensure that policy changes do not harm the most vulnerable in society and is central to international climate policy debates (ILO, 2015; Evans and Phelan, 2016; IPPR, 2019; UNFCCC, 2020a; Snell, 2022). In 2015 in the Paris Agreement, the term 'just transition' was used for the first time and was further mainstreamed within global climate policy in 2018 when 54 countries signed the 'Just transition declaration' at COP24

(Snell, 2022). Since 2015 the language of a just transition has been integral to Net Zero (and wider climate policy) discourse. The following quotation highlights the use of this terminology at the global level:

> A just transition means transforming the economy and economic system in a way that is as fair and inclusive as possible to everyone concerned, creating decent work opportunities and leaving no one behind. (United Nations, 2023)

The phrase 'leaving no one behind' has also become associated with discussions of a just transition, and both are used throughout climate negotiations and agreements. However, while the term 'just transition' has become widely used within policy circles, it is often used in a relatively narrow way, often with an implicit emphasis on 'workers and communities' perhaps reflecting the origins of the concept (see ILO, 2015; Just Transition Centre, 2017; UNRISD and ULIP, 2018). In this book we move beyond such a narrow focus on workers and jobs, reflecting our concern with justice as associated with a broader range of changes experienced by ordinary people in their everyday lives. Indeed, we argue that just climate futures are futures that offer fair opportunities to live, work, care and play, while also reducing emissions associated with climate change.

Towards just climate futures

Gaps in current thinking

Interestingly, while action *is* being taken towards Net Zero by nation states, the emphasis on a just transition appears to be lacking within policy frameworks, even under a relatively narrow understanding. Indeed, only a small number of governments – Canada, Germany, Scotland and Spain – have specific just transition initiatives (Robins, 2020: 8). Taking Scotland's approach to the transition as an example, it can be considered rare in two ways. First, it is one of the few countries that explicitly discusses a just transition; indeed, action at the UK level is far less advanced, with no explicit ambition of placing justice at the centre of its Net Zero work (IPPR, 2017). Second, and integral to this book, is that its understanding of the just transition goes beyond a narrow focus on jobs and places in which these jobs are based. Scotland recognizes other potential ways in which mitigation policies could be harmful to specific groups and communities such as changes to availability of transport infrastructure and the effects of green tariffs on the cost of living. We argue throughout this book that any policy discussion of a just transition needs to extend this approach even further, recognizing that the inequalities between place, context and socio-economic and demographic characteristics will affect how households are able to engage with the transition to Net Zero, and whether they face the risk of being left behind. Furthermore, we argue that a just transition must recognize inequalities between places, disparities within places, and even within households, and ensure that these are addressed and accounted for in both national and local policymaking and implementation.

Aside from policy, academic research that goes beyond the original narrow framing of the just transition as relevant to employment and the impacts on communities reliant on carbon intensive industries (UNFCCC, 2020a) *does* exist. Indeed, there is a growing literature that broadens this focus, addressing injustices associated with other areas of Net Zero policy. This includes work on home energy, mobility, food and leisure under Net Zero profiled in detail in Chapter 3. However, most of this work deals with one very specific aspect of everyday life at a time (for example, justice implications of smart heating systems, or electric vehicle charging). While this literature is extremely valuable (and indeed we discuss its usefulness in Chapter 3), the singular focus of most studies is in some respects problematic, as it does not provide insight into the multifaceted, interconnected, multi-layered changes that Net Zero policies are likely to bring. For example – the increased use of smart heating systems within the home will occur within the context of multiple other changes including other widespread changes within the home (such as a switch to heat pumps, changes to the type of energy used within the home, changes to physical heating infrastructure), within the world of work (for example, a gradual loss of 'brown' jobs in favour of 'green' jobs and associated need for training and reskilling), changes to mobility (such as the switch from ICE vehicles to EVs, the need for EV charging). We argue that focusing on one Net Zero change at a time means that the interactions and knock-on effects of these multiple changes are potentially masked. For example, if a household faces increased food or energy costs, this will impact on their spending on mobility or leisure. As such, the relatively atomized nature of both research and policy, and limited efforts to understand the effects of the transition on everyday life as a whole remains a significant gap in knowledge (Middlemiss et al, 2023), and one that is addressed within this book.

Further, while there is a significant literature base around the relationship between inequalities, injustices and policy areas relevant to Net Zero (such as the energy justice, mobilities and food insecurity literatures), there is relatively limited discussion of this in research and policy both relating to Net Zero itself and to the likely impacts of the changes it will bring. This is problematic given that existing social inequalities and divisions (gender, income, age, social class, housing tenure, disability, family structure, ethnicity and so on) are likely to have a significant impact on a person's ability to engage with Net Zero policies. For example, someone on a low income living in the private rented sector may encounter a range of barriers that prevent them from improving the energy efficiency of their home. While in the short term this may mean that they are unable to participate in the Net Zero agenda, in the medium to long term they risk being 'left behind', with outdated, expensive to maintain technology and infrastructure, and exposed to higher running costs as polluting technologies (such as fossil fuel powered boilers) are subject to higher taxation. At present, we argue that existing debates around Net Zero are too universal in terms of the vision of future life that they create, and fail to take existing inequalities into account. While these issues are addressed in a piecemeal way via the energy justice literature (for example), these remain too narrow in scope, and again, fail to consider people's lives holistically.

We started this book by showing how research from The Young Foundation found Net Zero to be a contentious and divisive issue. The current approach to this topic, as we show in Chapter 2, paints a homogeneous vision of a low carbon future, which fails to account for social and historical differences between people and places and their capacity to act. Logically, this is a risky strategy: if people do not see themselves represented in Net Zero, resistance to it is likely to build. Indeed, an 'anti-Net Zero' populist response is already emerging, with right wing political actors mobilizing against perceived injustices associated with the policy area (Paterson et al, 2024). Such a mobilization seems inevitable, but also risks being justified if we cannot show how everyone has a future in this agenda. As brought to light in the conversation between Tim Sahay and Chris Shaw, more attractive working-class futures must be devised, which go beyond just business as usual with new green technology, or worse (Sahay, 2024). Without a properly inclusive approach, which allows people to both own and shape the agenda, and which ensures that it will not do further harm, an anti-Net Zero movement will emerge to 'get back' at this policy (Lister, 2016).

Thinking differently: putting people and place at the heart of Net Zero

As we undertook the research that underpins this book, and we began to review Net Zero policies, we quickly recognized that the impacts of the transition were widespread and would affect households' everyday lives in a multitude of ways. However, it also became clear that too often, Net Zero policies are presented and critically analysed in the singular fashion described earlier, with little attention paid to the wider context that they operate within. They are also often framed in a relatively technical manner – reflecting their disciplinary and policy roots – for example, discussions about mobility are understandably discussed within the context of transport studies and policy.

This book resists such an approach, instead making people's daily lives and their life experiences its focus. Given this, we made the decision to take a deliberately bottom up and accessible characterization of life under Net Zero, focusing on six areas of life that are likely to change. These six areas of life are conceptualized as follows:

1. Where we live: shelter and warmth
2. Where we go: transport and mobility
3. What we eat: food
4. What we do for fun: leisure
5. What we buy: consumption
6. What we do for work: jobs

Our hope in taking this approach is that the multidisciplinary nature of our work is strengthened, and our arguments are more accessible. For example, 'Where we go' is conceptually something that can be understood by everyone whereas 'mobility' or 'transport' is less accessible and is value-laden given the different theoretical perspectives taken within the literature (see Chapter 3). Using the term 'where we go' allows our discussion to be grounded in people's lived experiences, and enables us to take a multidisciplinary approach, drawing from a broader literature base.

The interconnectedness of these areas of life, with individual, household and community characteristics is key to our understanding here. The way that changes in each area of life are experienced by individuals will be shaped by the unique characteristics of the household they are part of, and the features of their community, including social and geographic factors. For example, a rural dwelling household in a socially deprived community with limited community resources will have different mobility needs and will engage with changes in transport systems differently, compared to a wealthy household living in an urban area with existing excellent public transport links. Moreover, changes in one area of life will affect the ability of individuals, households and communities to participate in change in other areas.

It is also important to consider the central impact of place. Understanding the differences in how the journey to Net Zero will be mediated according to place-based and geographic factors and by the distribution of household profiles with varying needs within a place is critical in determining the best strategies to achieve – and accelerate – inclusive decarbonization. The variable resilience and preparedness of the UK's housing stock for energy efficiency and climate impacts is well known (Poruschi and Ambrey, 2018; Kelly et al, 2020), as is the challenge of localizing industries, economies and skills (Kapetaniou and McIvor, 2020); the burden of public service adaptation (HM Treasury, 2021), and the requirement for new or renewed green (transport, technology and energy) infrastructure (International Transport Forum, 2020). A transition to Net Zero requires a systemic, multi-layered shift to the infrastructure of place, to the quality of life and productivity that places can offer in a more localized world, and to the connectivity between places through low-carbon transport and logistics. Place will be critical in maintaining peoples' opportunities for mobility, prosperity and social connection.

In the UK, another dimension of inequalities in how we respond to the climate crisis is the increasingly uneven distribution of power. For example, in 2023, 300 councils in England had declared a climate emergency (LGA, 2022) yet the available budgets, devolution settlements and strength of local institutions to respond was significantly diminished through over a decade of cuts, budget freezes and austerity. The reality is that the distribution of disadvantaged households, infrastructure, services and assets across local places rarely matches up with the budgets and powers available to the local authority to achieve Net Zero. As Hoole et al (2023) put it: 'limited organisational capabilities of local institutions, together with a low-level of direct investment in regions, underpin a path-dependency, which makes it more difficult for the least productive, most deprived regions to change their growth trajectories' and furthermore 'undermine agility, responsiveness, and resilience in the face of shocks' (Hoole et al, 2023).

Thinking differently: starting in the present

In order to understand the potential impact of Net Zero policies we must understand overall distributions of environmental harm across the sum of these areas of life – in short – who is contributing most to climate change and in what ways, who is contributing the least, and where they live. Figure 1.1 shows the environmental impact of household consumption by income, divided into the first five areas of life we have identified (employment/work is excluded here as it does not involve households directly consuming carbon).

Figure 1.1 shows that environmental impact increases with income, with the wealthiest income group having a carbon footprint over two times larger that of the lowest. Not every area of life increases with income, for example, the carbon footprint of 'where we live' is around 6–7 tonnes per household for the first nine deciles. In contrast, 'where we go' and 'what we do for fun' are 2.5 and almost 4 times larger when comparing the lowest and highest income groups. This is in line with existing evidence that suggests a clear relationship between income and environmental impact, a trend that holds both within and between nations (Steinberger et al, 2010; Hubacek et al, 2017; Ivanova and Wood, 2020; Oswald et al, 2020; Owen and Barrett, 2020). Households that are wealthy spend the most on goods and services and have the largest environmental impacts. The link between carbon footprint and social deprivation has been shown to be a strong, inverse proportion (Owen and Kilian, 2019), meaning the higher the likelihood of deprivation the lower the carbon footprint is likely to be.

Figure 1.1: Equivalized two-adult household carbon footprints

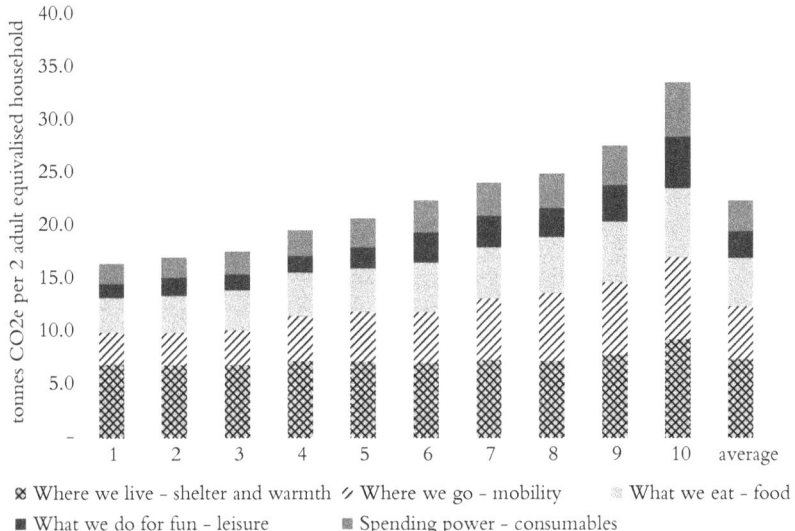

Note: The household spends have been equivalized for comparison to show the impact of a two-adult household in each decile, the standard household type used by the OECD and UK government when making comparisons by income decile.

Source: Data from University of Leeds (2021)

Researchers have also looked at how the contribution to climate change is patterned by place – with some types of neighbourhood having higher impacts than others (Druckman and Jackson, 2009). While there is a wealth and income story here: on average, people in 'prospering suburbs' are likely to be richer than those 'constrained by circumstance', there are also important considerations related to mobility and access to energy in rural versus urban contexts.

What this evidence base has given us to date, is a clear message that while the impacts of climate change are highly uneven, climate policies pose similar risks, especially where they fail to recognize existing inequalities. Our argument in this book is that it is essential to first understand these issues and their complexities, before attempting to find ways of addressing them. You would not pour concrete onto an uneven road and expect an even surface, without first filling in the gaps, cracks and traps which mean some areas of the road have less structural stability than others.

Thinking about trade-offs surrounding environmental policy is by no means new. There is substantial existing published literature that helps us begin to understand these risks. Long standing concerns about the potential tensions and trade-offs between social, environmental and economic policies have been raised in academic, policy and activist domains. It has become a central part of global climate policy debate, in part given long standing concerns about equity and justice enshrined in the 1987 Brundtland Report, and the post-2015 Paris emphasis on the just transition (Just Transition Centre, 2017; UNRISD and ULIP, 2018; UNFCCC, 2020a). The environment and climate justice movements and academic fields have also provided significant insights into the distributional impacts of climate change and climate policy, and the ways in which these can be mitigated (Robinson and Shine, 2018) as a starting point. The debate is also becoming increasingly common in fields that have previously resisted discussions about the environment – for example, in the field of social policy there has been substantial work considering these potential policy tensions – often falling under the umbrella terms of 'eco-social policy' and 'sustainable welfare' (Koch and Fritz, 2014; Bohnenberger, 2020; Zimmermann and Graziano, 2020; Gough, 2022, 2011; Mandelli, 2022; Snell et al, 2023).

Using the 'where we live' area of life as an example – there is a well-developed housing inequality and energy poverty literature base that highlights the health inequalities associated with living in poor housing conditions (Marmot et al, 2020; Ivanova and Middlemiss, 2021; Ballesteros-Arjona et al, 2022). These inequalities are intersections of poverty and low income, limited rights for tenants, poor housing conditions, and a range of other structural inequalities. Researchers working in the housing, fuel poverty, and Net Zero space also articulate that for a just transition to occur, multifaceted interventions are necessary, and that households are unlikely to be able to engage with these changes without significant support (both financial and practical) (Gillard et al, 2017; Ambrosio-Albala et al, 2020; Bartiaux et al, 2021; Owen et al, 2023). Moreover, the fuel poverty and housing literature warns about the unintentional introduction of new inequalities, for example the substantial emphasis on increased future use of smart technology has raised significant concerns about a widening digital divide (Martiskainen et al, 2021; Sovacool et al, 2021).

We want to be clear here that there are also significant opportunities in the Net Zero agenda for a more equal society, leading to a transformative rather than a replicative effect, and again, we restate our belief in this as an outcome. How we achieve this is the focus of Chapters 4 and 5. However, Chapters 2 and 3 systematically build a picture of the inequalities associated with each of the areas of life discussed here.

Some important clarifications

The climate crisis as a human crisis

We cannot jump into a book about mitigating climate change without first articulating some of the climate science behind the changes anticipated, and how these link to human life. We do not dwell on these in the rest of the book, however they provide an important backdrop to discussions of the just transition. The human causes of climate change (anthropogenic climate change) are largely attributed to greenhouse gas emissions linked to economic changes associated with the industrial revolution and ensuing consumer society, and are associated with activities such as: generating power, manufacturing goods, cutting down forests, using transportation, producing food, powering buildings and over consumption (UN, 2024b). The effects of these activities are outlined in Box 1.2.

Box 1.2: The causes of anthropogenic climate change

Anthropogenic greenhouse gas emissions have increased since the pre-industrial era, driven largely by economic and population growth, and are now higher than ever. This has led to atmospheric concentrations of carbon dioxide, methane and nitrous oxide that are unprecedented in at least the last 800,000 years. Their effects, together with those of other anthropogenic drivers, have been detected throughout the climate system and are extremely likely to have been the dominant cause of the observed warming since the mid-20th century.

IPCC, 2018: 4

It is important to note at this stage that there is scientific consensus around some of the fundamental elements of climate change. Most notably, that human activity is causing climate change (also referred to throughout the literature as anthropogenic climate change or global warming). Oreskes first identified this in her 2004 paper considering the stance of 928 refereed journal papers on climate change, finding that 'none of the papers disagreed with the consensus position' (Oreskes, 2004). Later, in a 2013 study, Cook et al (2013) reviewed 11,944 climate abstracts between 1991 and 2011, and found that only a 'miniscule proportion of the published research, with the percentage decreasing over time' rejected the idea of anthropogenic global warming (AGW), compared to 97 per cent endorsed the scientific consensus (2013: 6).

In March 2022, the IPCC's latest report found that unless carbon emissions peaked by 2025 and reduced by 43 per cent by 2030, it would be impossible to avoid the human, social, financial and environmental catastrophe caused by global temperature rises of more than 1.5 degrees (IPCC, 2022). Globally, the consequences of climate change are stark, with rising temperatures, sea levels and increased climatic events presenting substantial risks to human health, livelihoods and ultimately survival (see Table 1.1 for an overview of these).

Table 1.1: Overview of the threats to human life created by climate change

Threats	Cause of threat
Health	Heat related illness and death; injury/loss of life associated with severe weather events; vector-borne/water-borne diseases, exacerbation of cardiovascular/respiratory diseases through air pollution; mental trauma from displacement/loss of livelihoods and property.
Food and water	Losses to crops and livestock as a result of flooding and drought. Also increased soil degradation which has further impacts on crop productivity. Climate variability and extreme weather among drivers of rise in global hunger. Impacts on fisheries as a result of increased temperatures and salinity.
Property, security and livelihoods	Loss of agricultural livelihoods as described earlier. Increased conflict. Internal disaster displacements between January and June 2019 (close to 22 million in total for 2019). Displacement across borders also occurs, and may be interrelated with other reasons for migration, such as conflict. Lake Chad region has seen movement of millions of people across borders (due to environmental deterioration, water scarcity and mismanagement, population increase, scarce resources and conflict). Loss of property, livelihoods and financial security as a result of migration.

Source: Adapted from Snell (2022) drawing on WMO (2018: 27–32), and Robinson and Shine (2018)

While the most severe impacts of climate change often affect the poorest people in the poorest places (Robinson and Shine, 2018), with low lying developing countries at high risk of the negative impacts, climate change and related policy affects everyone. In the UK, for example, there is extensive evidence that links climate change to increased flooding and coastal erosion with associated damage to properties and infrastructure including energy supply; pressures on water quality and resources; biodiversity, soil and land use impacts. These have significant impacts on both the capacity to provide clean water, energy and emergency responses, run public services, and, more directly, on human health (Environment Agency, 2022). Readers interested in deepening their understanding of the science of climate change should follow the work of the UNFCCC.

A note on conceptual clarity

As committed interdisciplinarians we are eclectic in our reading, and we are keen to draw on a range of inputs rooted in different theoretical traditions. A more bounded disciplinary approach would argue for one concept above others, and stick with theories and empirical work that relate only to that concept. We avoid this form of conceptual purity as it would require us to read much more narrowly, and offer a less full account of the evidence. The environmental social sciences are an interdisciplinary endeavour, and scholars in these fields (including ourselves) draw on a wide range of concepts to articulate the risks associated with increasing inequality or reproducing injustice.

So, what are the concepts in use here? One group of concepts comes from the Bristol Social Exclusion Matrix (B-SEM) framework, which is associated with social exclusion, describing this in relation to people's access to resources, ability to participate in society, and ability to achieve a quality of life (Levitas et al, 2007). We explain our choice of B-SEM as a framework in Chapter 4. While it has become central in the way that we articulate our work, social exclusion is one of a number of concepts that describe a problem in society. This problem is also sometimes described as an injustice, an inequality or as a form of poverty, which results from one or other vulnerability. Each of these terms has a slightly different meaning, as well as belonging to a different theoretical tradition. Justice and injustice, for instance, have a strong normative flavour: implying that the current order of the world is wrong and must be corrected. From an environmental perspective these are widely used in relation to climate, energy and environment more generally, and have long been associated with work on climate futures (Robinson and Shine, 2018). This is partly why we called our book *'Just' Climate Futures*.

As readers we encourage you to espouse this eclectic approach, not least because there are excellent and useful ideas in all of these traditions that will help us to come towards a better journey to Net Zero. While we prioritize 'social inclusion', we acknowledge a debt to those using different terminology, and attempt to pay them due respect in building our arguments here.

Project team and use of empirical data

As described in the Preface, this text is based on an empirical project 'Understanding family and community vulnerabilities in transition to Net Zero' funded by the Nuffield Foundation. The project drew together a multi-disciplinary team of researchers. This allowed us to approach the issue of Net Zero and the just transition in new, uncharted ways, and it also provided (as discussed previously), new theoretical perspectives about how to understand issues of inequality and (in)justice within the transition. Over the course of the project we collected substantial amounts of qualitative data, working with people from seven low-income neighbourhoods in Leeds and Newcastle, UK, to understand perspectives on the planned policies for Net Zero, and how they were able to engage with this agenda. The seven neighbourhoods in Leeds and Newcastle were chosen as case study locations in recognition that the impact of the transition in the UK will vary regionally, with particular concern for Yorkshire and the North of England (IPPR, 2019). While this data is not the focus of this book, indeed, it can be accessed in Middlemiss et al (2024), we draw on quotations and other forms of data throughout the book to bring issues around justice, inequality, and the Net Zero transition to life.

We end this chapter with a brief note on our position as authors. As social scientists working in the field of climate change, we are passionate about taking action to both mitigate, and to enable society to adapt to, its effects. We are also convinced that the public conversation on this topic has to date been too little concerned with the challenges of ensuring that both the outcomes and delivery of such action is fair, and that climate policy takes into account people's different starting points and needs. At the time of writing we are experiencing both a climate emergency and a cost of living crisis. We collectively believe that both can be addressed simultaneously, and that a just transition that leaves no one behind is entirely possible. It is our hope that this book can refresh this debate, providing a roadmap to a truly just transition to Net Zero.

What to expect in the rest of the book

In this book we address the gaps in knowledge outlined earlier, reframing the just transition debate to put people and their everyday lives at its centre. In doing so we understand how Net Zero will affect people's lives as a whole, as well as recognizing that existing social arrangements, inequalities and injustices will shape how people will experience these complex, multi-layered policy changes. We propose an analytical framework to identify the risks of exclusion under envisaged transitions to Net Zero. We hope that researchers and policymakers can use this framework to identify who is most at risk of exclusion during the transition, and design policy to reduce exclusion.

This book is organized across five chapters. Chapters 2 and 3 explore the policy changes associated with Net Zero, and associated challenges to ensure a 'just transition'. Chapter 4 then presents a new way of thinking about the relationship between inequalities, social inclusion and Net Zero, drawing heavily on the concept of social inclusion, and the B-SEM framework (described previously). Indeed, the chapter adapts the B-SEM framework to draw together social and environmental thinking in a new way that highlights the risks associated with the transition more comprehensively and holistically. Chapter 5 then shows how this new way of thinking can be used to ensure a 'just climate future', presenting a practical roadmap for policymakers and practitioners that will help design and implement climate policy in a more socially just, place appropriate way.

2

Net Zero Policy and Climate Futures

*Carolyn Snell, Lucie Middlemiss, Kelli Kennedy,
Tania Carregha and Anne Owen*

Introduction

As is becoming clear from our discussion so far, Net Zero policies are likely to bring about widespread societal change, both on a technical level – in terms of the infrastructure and technology we use, and on a social level, in terms of how we interact and engage with this changing landscape. Chapter 1 has alluded to some of these changes and the cumulative, intersecting impacts on our daily lives, both now, and at different points in the future as policy changes gather momentum. Further, it has highlighted the significant gaps in knowledge about the nature of these changes and how they will affect different people differently.

This chapter begins to expand on the six identified areas of everyday life that are likely to be significantly affected by Net Zero policies (Figure 2.1). As explained in Chapter 1, the terminology used throughout this chapter reflects the everyday lived experience of these issues rather than the more technical and/or theoretical language used across policy and academic debates. The images in Figure 2.1 bring life to this point, illustrating, in our participants' words (and images), how their daily lives interact with different aspects of Net Zero. Here our participants talked about their lives as a whole – discussing transport in the context of needing a car to get to work, socialize, or buy food, discussing home energy in the context of working from home, and so on.

Figure 2.1: Daily interactions with Net Zero policies

Summarizing key areas of change – visions of a Net Zero future

The analysis undertaken in this chapter has been informed by the most prominent discussions of life under Net Zero that exist within the public domain in the UK (referred to throughout this book as 'visions') – these have been developed and discussed by the Climate Change Committee (CCC) (Climate Change Committee, 2020a, 2020b) and the Department for Business, Energy, and Industrial Strategy (BEIS)[1] (BEIS, 2021a, 2021b) which provide regular, thorough analysis. Citizen-led policy work via the Climate Assembly (Climate Assembly UK, 2020), and academics from the Centre for Research into Energy Demand Solutions (CREDS) (Barrett et al, 2021) have also presented visions of future Net Zero life. These 'visions' of the future are summarized in Table 2.1 and afterwards explained in detail, using the future focused and sometimes aspirational language of their proponents. We also provide examples of Net Zero policies already in place through a series of tables in each section (Tables 2.2 to 2.7).

Following this we begin the discussion about the *just transition* – considering the potential risks of Net Zero policies if they are pursued without recognition of existing social divisions. Chapter 3 then presents a full analysis of the risks and opportunities of Net Zero policy across these different areas of life.

While our work has been informed by UK research and policy, it is important to note that these visions of the future and ways of achieving them are largely consistent across the Global North. This is because they are frequently described in technical and policy terms, and as a result tend to profile certain technologies, tried and tested methods of reducing carbon, and well-established policy instruments to achieve this (for example, financial incentives to encourage take up of home insulation or electric vehicles, spending on infrastructure to improve walking and cycling) (OECD, 2022). Where these do differ between

Table 2.1: Key changes associated with the Net Zero transition

Area of daily life	Visions of the future (distilled from key references)
Where we live	More localized energy systems – such as heat networks; increased micro generation, home or community based solar; greater electricity use for heating/cooking, including more heat pumps (electric heating); use of hydrogen as a home energy source; increased use of smart home technology and systems (such as smart meters and appliances); increased home energy efficiency (insulation and efficient appliances); more flexible use of energy (such as time of use tariffs).
Where we go	Move to electric vehicles (EVs), phasing out cars with an internal combustion engine (ICE); encouraging and providing infrastructure for active travel (walking and cycling); providing green public transport.
What we eat	Eating less meat; reduced food waste and carbon footprint (reducing road miles, packaging); changed agricultural practices to reduce emissions.
What we do for fun	Travel less and enjoy leisure activities locally, or virtually; increased green leisure and active travel; reduced high carbon footprint leisure (reducing flying and car miles).
What we spend our money on	Some products become more expensive as a result of carbon taxes/pricing, others become cheaper; increased standards and regulations result in some goods being discontinued, unusable or banned; from fast to slow fashion; more second-hand markets, repair and reuse; reduction of waste.
What we do for work	More jobs in the green economy; fewer jobs in carbon-based industries (such as mining, steel); new skills for green work; increased homeworking.

Source: Based on BEIS (2021a); CREDS et al (2021); Climate Assembly UK (2020); CCC (2021, 2020a, 2020b). Reproduced from: Middlemiss et al (2023). Reproduced with permission of The Licensor through PLSclear.

countries it is largely as a result of the political context of a particular country. For example, policy approaches in Norway are grounded in its unique position as one of the world's largest energy exporters (Malka et al, 2023) and decarbonization of the automotive industry in Germany is politically sensitive given the historic size of the sector (Mazur et al, 2015). While our initial discussion further on is based on UK visions of the future, we supplement this discussion with further national and international examples.

Note also that this chapter steps back somewhat from our goal to 'put people and place at the heart of Net Zero', in that it describes the current rather homogenized vision of the future, in which people's starting points and differences are not accounted for. We begin to remedy this homogeneity from Chapter 3 onwards.

Areas of daily life: where we live

The nature of the change

This area of life considers where and how we live, including the home we live in, and the resources we use within it. We first consider what these technical changes are most likely to be, the policy instruments used to implement them, and the broad impact on people's lives (this will be discussed in more detail in Chapter 3).

A significant predicted change is the move towards greater electricity use within the home. In terms of heating, we are likely to see a shift away from natural gas to the use of heat pumps, electric heating and heat networks. Homes are likely to be 'smarter' with heating and lighting controls that enable greater energy efficiency. While new builds will be built to high energy efficiency standards, older housing will need to be extensively retrofitted to ensure energy efficiency, and the electrical items we use within the home will also be more energy efficient. Energy itself may become more decentralized, with greater emphasis on local generation of renewables, and local energy networks.

Making it happen

A range of policy instruments is likely to be used including changes in the regulation of energy and housing markets to incentivize improved energy efficiency, substantial public and private investment in retrofit, changes in local government powers/planning laws to allow (for example) heat networks and the microgeneration of energy, and measures to support behavioural change.

Market based instruments will place penalties on high carbon housing/consumer goods, and generate incentives for low carbon housing/consumer goods. This could include changes to stamp duty, changed regulation within the electricity market (Climate Change Committee, 2020a, 2020b), and changes to VAT[2] on low carbon heating products (Climate Assembly UK, 2020). Domestic Energy Performance Certificates (EPCs) could be adjusted to provide a greater emphasis on 'positive energy use', and energy tariffs could be restructured to incentivize this – for example, reductions in use, or use during off peak periods (Climate Change Committee, 2020a, 2020b).

It is also predicted that there will be changes in terms of the governance and provision of home energy, with greater emphasis on local heat networks, the promotion of area-based energy plans, and the zoning of heat networks. Here local government and community organizations may have a greater role than they had previously. All the visions of the future discuss behavioural change, from getting householders engaged with smart heating management (Climate Change Committee, 2020a, 2020b; Barrett et al, 2021), smart lighting controls (Barrett et al, 2021), through to more radical changes such as increased household occupancy/co-housing (Barrett et al, 2021).

By means of international comparison and to demonstrate the similarities of policies across nations, some examples of policy targets in place at the time of writing across the Global North are provided in Table 2.2. As indicated, the targets and policy measures are very similar, focusing on retrofit, changes

Table 2.2: Where we live: examples of relevant policies

Area	Examples of policies and targets
UK	The UK currently prohibits the renting out of privately owned domestic properties with poor energy efficiency (EPC rating E and lower) (DESNZ, 2023). Additionally, it uses market based instruments to pay for domestic home improvements and retrofit via the Energy Company Obligation (UK Government, 2024). Current energy efficiency policy targets are as follows: • new buildings to be zero carbon by 2025 • all new homes to be EPC 'C' or above by 2028 • new boilers to be hydrogen ready by 2025 • home oil and coal phase out by 2033 • heat pump roll out aiming for more than 1 million sales by 2030 • increased energy efficiency measures to include: 700,000 new loft insulations by 2025; 200,000 new cavity wall insulations by 2025; 250,000 new solid wall insulations by 2025 (Climate Change Committee, 2020a)
Germany	The German Federal government has created legislation that prevents installation of pure oil heating systems if more climate friendly options are available; with a complete ban on fossil fuel by 2045 (The Federal Government, 2020). Tax relief for energy efficient renovation (tax payable reduced by 20 per cent) is provided including low interest loans of up to €120,000. It has the following relevant Net Zero targets: • overall plan to drop emissions of the building sector by two thirds by 2030 • phase out of installations of pure oil heating systems by 2026 • 65 per cent renewable heating in new buildings from 2024 • renovation of 64 per cent housing stock by 2033 (based on EU targets) (The Federal Government, 2020)
US	There is substantial state level legislation across the US supporting Net Zero policies. For example, New York has legislation 'Local Law 97' that limits carbon emissions by building size – requires 40 per cent citywide emissions reductions from the 2005 baseline by 2030. There is also financial support, for example, in Massachusetts the Governor announced creation of Massachusetts Community Climate Bank in 2023, the $50m state seeded fund to support affordable housing markets' energy transition. There are also policy targets in place across the US, with the following announced in California: • 6 million heat pumps to be deployed by 2030 in California • 3 million 'climate friendly' homes by 2030 • 7 million 'climate friendly' homes by 2035 including: improved energy efficiency, a move from gas to electricity, addition of solar and battery storage systems, better ventilation. Emphasis on the need to improve older homes (Governor Newsom's Office, 2022)

in fuel type and renewables, with public spending, regulation and market-based instruments (such as carbon taxes) all used to achieve these goals.

Impacting people

It is clear from this analysis that the transition to Net Zero will significantly alter the way we light, heat, occupy space and even cook within the home. Net Zero visions within this area of life are broadly similar to each other in terms of what changes we should expect, but differ according to their ambition and proposed timeframes. While discussed in detail in Chapter 3, in broad terms, these changes are likely to change relationships between households and energy providers, introduce a greater emphasis on and requirement to use technology within the home and to significantly change daily routines and practices (Shove and Walker, 2014). As such, the impact of these changes on households across time and space should not be underestimated.

Areas of daily life: where we go

The nature of the change

Here we consider where we go, when we go there, and how, considering transport systems and infrastructure, along with the way in which goods and services are both provided and accessed. Note that we leave discussion of air travel here to the 'what we do for fun' section.

Net Zero-related changes will have a substantial impact on both transport systems and our mobility. There is substantial emphasis on transport systems within official Net Zero policies, with changes likely to affect private cars, motorbikes and vans, through to HGVs, trains and buses. In the UK, like many other developed countries, a cornerstone of Net Zero policy is the phasing out of cars with an internal combustion engine (ICE) in favour of electric vehicles (EVs). For example, in the UK it is expected that by 2035[3] new ICE cars and vans will be banned, with hybrid vehicles following a similar timeline and replaced with EVs or hydrogen vehicles. Note that this potentially brings together 'where we live' and 'where we go' in people's everyday life, obfuscating the divisions between these two. Specifically, where people have an EV and can charge at home, the costs of both will be reflected in the electricity bill, and this will offer the potential for the use of EVs as battery storage.

Alongside the shift to low carbon vehicles is the proposed improvement of active travel and public transport, including the increased use of e-scooters and e-bikes. There are calls for cycle lanes and walking routes to be improved in support of active travel, making it safer and more desirable. There is an emphasis on the role of localism and local government across the different visions of Net Zero, for example, local transport policies will need to be more integrated – with both investment in public transport and active travel, and support for EV charging necessary. There is also a call for more community owned/supported transport including both public transport and car clubs.

There is disagreement between the visions of the future when it comes to road building – some, for example CREDS (Barrett et al, 2021) would prefer to see no substantial new roads or airports. Indeed, in the non-governmental visions of life under Net Zero we see efforts made to reduce travel and private car ownership, with an increase in working at home and video conferencing (and associated improvements to broadband speeds and technology), more car sharing, a reduction in multiple vehicle ownership, and more 'low transport' neighbourhoods. However, this is less common within governmental policy narratives, and is also criticized by organizations representing members of the public. For example, the UK's Climate Assembly supports improvements to public transport and active travel, but opposes any changes that impose restrictions on people's lives (Climate Assembly UK, 2020).

Making it happen

Regardless of the exact nature of the changes implemented, there are a number of key policy instruments that will be used, most notably: regulation, investment, strengthened local planning powers, market-based instruments, and behavioural measures. Change to vehicle use is likely to occur through: banning sales of new ICE vehicles, the gradual decommissioning of ICE vehicles (promoted through scrappage schemes), subsidies for EVs and home charging points, investment in the non-home based charging infrastructure including incentives for employers, local authority investment in local charging infrastructure, and changes to local planning laws and other regulations to encourage EV use (such as the use of traffic regulations to allow preferential parking), and investment in public and active transport. In order to change behaviour and reduce travel, investment in broadband is required to encourage home working, alongside investment in community car clubs, and campaigns to promote active travel, reduced numbers of private vehicle journeys and car sharing.

Again, examples of various policies are provided in Table 2.3 – as with the previous section, the targets and policy measures are very similar to each other. It is interesting to note that the ICE phase out across the EU has been controversial, with Germany, a country whose economy is heavily based on the automotive industry successfully pushing for a series of exemptions (Martinez et al, 2023).

Table 2.3: Where we go: examples of relevant policies

Area	Examples of policies and targets
UK	The UK (as with EU countries) has a ban on new ICE vehicles by 2035 and has the following policy targets: • 80 per cent of new cars and 70 per cent of new vans sold in the UK to be zero emission by 2030, increasing to 100 per cent by 2035 • by 2030 'We will aim to have half of all journeys in towns and cities cycled or walked' • 'Ambition for all diesel-only trains to be removed from the network by 2040' (DfT, 2021a) The government is also investing in active transport networks (see for example (Active Travel England, 2024).
Europe	EU with legislation is in place to ban new ICE vehicles, and to extend charging infrastructure. Specific EU targets are: • new ICE cars banned by 2035 • provision of EV charging stations every 60 km on major roads by 2025 (European Parliament, 2022) There is also substantial policy change across EU countries. For example, Sweden is moving towards a 'transport-efficient society' through improving access to efficient, punctual and reliable public transport, shifting to less energy-intensive vehicles, higher use of vehicle capacity, and increased use of rail and sea transport, among other measures. Public spending on public transport and active travel infrastructure has also been increased, alongside the introduction of higher rates of taxation for carbon emitting vehicles and subsidies for those with low emissions (again, see Sweden for example: UNFCCC, 2020b).
North America	Canada has similar legislation and targets to those in Europe: • phase out of new passenger ICE vehicles by 2035 • manufacturers targets for EV/hybrid production: 20 per cent in 2026; 23 per cent in 2027; 34 per cent by 2028; 43 per cent by 2029; 60 per cent by 2030 (CBC News, 2023) In the US, while resisting a ban on ICE vehicles, the state of Colorado aims to phase out gasoline powered vehicles by 2050, using tax incentives to encourage the purchase of EVs (both domestic and trucks), an e-bike programme giving away 10,000 e-bikes to low-income residents by 2025, and investing in the charging network (Colorado Energy Office, 2023).

Impacts

Net Zero policy discussions in this area suggest substantial changes to the way we travel, where we go, how often we take these journeys, or whether we travel to access goods and services at all. Overall, depth of change and ambition varies across the visions of the future with some, for example Barrett et al (2021) emphasizing reduced travel and behavioural change, and others including the CCC and Citizen's Assembly highlighting the significance of EVs to the transition. Given that policy narratives tend to focus on transitions in private transport (that is, from ICE to EV), it is likely that these changes will be most prominent, although changes to local planning and public transport, and the promotion of active travel, are also highly likely. These changes are likely to have multiple impacts on households, these impacts are likely to grow over time, and intersect with other areas of daily life – for example, the availability of transport shapes our employment prospects alongside our ability to gain education and training, and to fulfil other needs such as accessing affordable food).

Areas of daily life: what we eat

The nature of the change

Our focus here is the food that is available to us, what we are encouraged to eat, how we manage food waste, and how food is produced and transported. Net Zero policies are predicted to affect food systems, with significant changes predicted between the publication of this text and 2050. While our emphasis here is the impact of Net Zero policies on people's everyday lives, it is also important to recognize that the changing climate itself is likely to affect which crops are able to grow in the UK, and the stability of supply chains in the UK and internationally, meaning that certain foods or food types will not be accessible or will become more expensive (Climate Change Committee, 2021).

At present a number of aspects of food production[4] and consumption are associated with high carbon emissions. The red meat and dairy industry have an especially high carbon footprint, and there is emphasis across the different visions of Net Zero of a change in diets away from carbon intensive food such as this. For example, different visions of Net Zero paint a range of possible future diets: ranging from many more people adopting plant-based diets (veganism), to people swapping red meat for white meat or fish, or dairy for legume consumption (Barrett et al, 2021). Given the carbon emissions associated with the transport of food, there is also emphasis in visions of Net Zero on people eating seasonally and locally or adopting location-appropriate diets (Kim et al, 2020).

Moreover, in the near future households will be encouraged to reduce food waste (Climate Change Committee, 2020a, 2020b). The public sector in the UK is expected to take the lead in reducing food waste (Climate Change Committee, 2021), and there is anticipated target setting on this in public and household sectors (Climate Change Committee, 2021, 2020a, 2020b).

There are also opportunities for changes in supply chains – for example by increasing the technological support around online shopping and home delivery, and moving towards centralized retail and distribution (Barrett et al, 2021).

Making it happen

Much of the shift in diets is assumed to come about in a voluntary way, with people being encouraged, persuaded, and 'nudged' to modify their diet to ensure reduced emissions, and to reduce the levels of food wasted (Climate Change Committee, 2020a, 2020b). Ideas vary on how to promote these behaviours, including 'climate labelling' on foods indicating their climate impact (Gadema and Oglethorpe, 2011), and the importance of the public sector (including schools) leading by example in this area.

Managing household food waste can also be addressed in part through 'nudge' techniques but can also be supported through government spending and provision such as food waste collection (Climate Change Committee, 2020b: 157). Policy examples are given in Table 2.4. Unlike other policy areas, innovation and Net Zero targets are often common within industry, for example, with major supermarkets developing their own targets via Corporate Social Responsibility initiatives, and with numerous voluntary commitments in place. France is perhaps an outlier with state driven policy in this area.

Table 2.4: What we eat: examples of relevant policies

Area	Examples of policies and targets
UK	The UK's Courtauld Commitment 2030 (supported by both government and industry) is a voluntary agreement across the UK food supply chain that aims to reduce environmental impacts. At present it has the following targets: • to deliver a 50 per cent per capita reduction in food waste by 2030 vs the UK 2007 baseline (covering manufacture, retail, hospitality and food service, and household) • to deliver a 50 per cent absolute reduction in GHG emissions associated with food and drink consumed in the UK by 2030 (against a 2015 baseline) • an overall target by 2030 that 50 per cent of fresh food is sourced from areas with sustainable water management (WRAP, 2024)
France	In 2016 legislation forbidding the destruction of unsold food from supermarkets that has the potential to be donated, as a food waste initiative – the 'Garot Law' was introduced. In addition, France has a target of reducing food waste by 50 per cent by 2025 (Zero Waste Europe, 2020).
Multinational	Multinational organizations often set their own Net Zero targets, Nestle for example aims to reduce its emissions by: • 20 per cent by 2025, from its baseline of 2018, and then • 50 per cent by 2030 These targets were developed with the support of the 'science based targets initiative'. In pursuit of these targets Nestle reports investing CHF3.2 billion (US$3.59 billion at the prevailing exchange rate) on measures 'that "advance" regenerative agriculture among its suppliers and a move to 100 percent renewable electricity by 2025' (Just Food, 2024).

Indeed, corporate power within the food industry is noteworthy as it is a potential challenge to policymaking. Work in this area warns us that there is a potential – and real – risk of corporate power being consolidated rather than challenged during the transition to Net Zero (Clapp et al, 2021; Slater et al, 2022). Technology-based, market solutions can potentially lead towards large corporate agri-business directing industry transformation towards their own strengths and benefits, such as technological solutions of gene editing, biotechnology, synthetic fertilizers and herbicides (Clapp and Ruder, 2020). Policymakers may find that they have to push back against the structural, instrumental, and discursive powers of transnational food corporations (Clapp and Scrinis, 2017) and the like in order to steer the food sector move towards Net Zero to be a just one that does not primarily benefit these corporate actors. This tension between corporate power shaping the path to Net Zero via technology, individual responsibility narratives towards diet changes, and government role towards agenda-setting towards Net Zero will prove to be a tightrope for policy and regulation moving forward.

Impacts

While changes within agriculture and food systems may affect food prices and availability, and households are likely to be actively encouraged to reduce and recycle food waste, the extent to which dietary change will be encouraged and will take place is harder to predict, given that it is such an emotive, personalized issue (and one where governments are often reluctant to intervene). However, as will be explored further in Chapter 3, customers are limited or encouraged in making certain choices based on what retailers offer (British Dietetic Association, 2021; Dimbleby, 2021; The Food Foundation, 2021), hence if Net Zero friendly options are not affordable or accessible, consumers' choices will be skewed or limited.

Areas of daily life: what we do for fun

The nature of the change

This area of life includes leisure activities, entertainment, recreation spaces such as green spaces, urban parks and national parks, tourism (including flying) and digital leisure.

Predicted Net Zero policy changes in this area are fragmented and often vague in nature, with some areas of policy more developed than others. For example, the policy debate around aviation tax is significantly developed compared to policy discussions around digital leisure. At present visions of the future consider several key areas. First, there is emphasis on the significance of protecting, creating and re-developing green space,[5] for example, the UK's Climate Change Committee (2021) advocates for the development of parks and woodlands within both urban and rural communities. Second, there is greater emphasis on localization, where communities are likely to be encouraged to access leisure and related amenities more locally than they currently do, thus avoiding more travel-intensive options (Climate Change Committee, 2021). Third, significant discussion exists around reducing air travel, especially for leisure, with an emphasis on the role of lower carbon forms of transport. Overall, air travel is likely to become more expensive, in part because of policies that penalize its use. This will have implications for people's choice in holiday destinations. Less apparent within visions of the future is the role of digital leisure as an alternative means of reducing leisure transport miles, however, there are proponents of its expansion as a Net Zero policy. Indeed, the pandemic brought to the fore the potential for virtual tourism, gaming, and online entertainment, and this is now discussed in terms of its usefulness for reducing our carbon emissions (see for example Scheer, 2023).

Making it happen

Policy changes are likely to come about in a number of ways: government spending is likely to be required to invest in public greenspaces (Climate Change Committee, 2021). Similarly, investment is also necessary to improve existing cycling and scootering infrastructure (Climate Change Committee, 2021; see also 'where we go', discussed previously) to enable people to make the most of their locality, and to make these activities more appealing as leisure activities in their own right. Investment in the provision of local opportunities for leisure and socializing is also critical here: not all neighbourhoods currently have an infrastructure for 'having fun'. Financial mechanisms such as aviation tax are already in place, and predictions are that these will be developed further in order to incentivize low-carbon travel, with taxation increasing as people fly more often and further (Climate Change Committee, 2021). There is an ongoing debate about the role of personal carbon allowances (see Fuso Nerini et al, 2021) as these may be used to further shape people's leisure activities. Table 2.5 highlights policy targets and policy instruments already in place across various countries.

Impacts

Under Net Zero, what people do for fun will be largely dependent on the same factors shaping the use of free time now, including accessibility, affordability and awareness. It will also be shaped by Net Zero policy, for instance by measures to conserve and expand green spaces, urban parks and national parks, with some gaining access to spaces not previously available.

Table 2.5: What we do for fun: examples of relevant policies

Area	Examples of policies and targets
US	The Los Angeles Mayor has set a range of leisure related Net Zero targets including: • to ensure that the proportion of Los Angelenos living within half a mile of a park or open space is at least 65 per cent by 2025; 75 per cent by 2035; and 100 per cent by 2050 • increase tree canopy in areas of greatest need by at least 50 per cent by 2028 • complete or initiate restoration identified in the 'ARBOR Plan' by 2035 • create a fully connected LARiverWay public access system that includes 32 miles of bike paths and trails by 2028 In support of this state funding for free plants and trees for residents to support the tree canopy target has been provided (City Plants, 2020), and the state is investing in the development of the LA River Way active travel network (Institute for Sustainable Infrastructure, 2023).
Iceland	Iceland's Prime Minister announced the reintroduction of a tourist tax in January 2024 to support environmental preservation and Net Zero initiatives, with funds being used to invest in (for example) public transport infrastructure and to repair damage caused by tourism. Multiple schemes exist within the country to support Net Zero policies, including voluntary measures to encourage tourists to offset their carbon emissions by donating to carbon capture programmes (Visit Iceland, 2024), and voluntary certification schemes for businesses to reward and publicize green credentials (Vakinn, 2024).
EU/ Norway	The European Union has introduced an emissions trading system, including aviation. All airlines operating in Europe are required to monitor, report and verify their emissions. Airlines receive tradable allowances for emissions per year (European Commission, 2024). At the time of writing Norway was the only EU country that levied a climate tax on domestic flights. In its Climate Plan, it proposes increasing the carbon tax in the run up to 2030 to support emission reductions (Norwegian Ministry of Climate and Environment, 2022).
France	Significant work was undertaken to reduce the carbon footprint of the 2024 Paris Olympics by half. At the time of writing, significant investment had been made to ensure the use of low carbon construction materials, use of solar and renewables to power events, smart design to reduce materials used and reduce waste, and re-use of materials post event (International Olympic Committee, 2023).

Some aspects of this area of life (such as tourism) overlap significantly with other areas of life – namely 'where we go'. Besides travel, leisure has large overlaps with 'what we buy'. With labour markets in transition and the pricing of a range of products and services potentially increasing, people may feel more financially restricted. Any spending on leisure activities may be the first to get cut from people's expenses.

Areas of daily life: what we buy

The nature of the change

This area of life considers how and what we purchase, the production of goods we buy and interact with, and how this might change in relation to Net Zero policies.

Net Zero policies are likely to bring about changes in pricing as carbon intensive products are subject to various forms of increased taxation/tariffs, and low carbon products are (initially) subject to subsidies. Net Zero policies may also bring with them improvements in product standards, meaning that products perform better, meet higher safety standards, last longer, need replacing less often and can be more easily repaired (Climate Assembly UK, 2020; Climate Change Committee, 2020a, 2020b). Net Zero related policies are likely to lead to some products being banned or altered, for example, certain refrigerators will be banned under new regulations on the use of 'F-gases' (Climate Change Committee, 2020a, 2020b). Raw materials in industries such as fashion are also likely to be reworked to be lower in carbon output, such as human-made cellulose fibres and animal fibres (Suresh, 2023; Taheraly et al, 2023).

One popular vision of the future is that consumers will be encouraged to keep goods for longer and move away from current modes of purchasing from the newest collections or fashion seasons, and replacing tech products before they have reached the end of their life (Barrett et al, 2021). Some predict an increased use of second-hand market platforms in clothing and textiles, packaging, vehicles, electronics, appliances and machinery and furniture, and incentives for consumers to use 'libraries of things', moving households away from ownership of goods such as tools and equipment and towards renting (Barrett et al, 2021). Furthermore, there is strong support for 'repair cafes' and 'skills swap shops' and other similar platforms that can help households to increase the life of goods and upskill the population in repair practices (Climate Assembly UK, 2020).

It is also predicted that waste will be drastically reduced with an intention of zero avoidable waste being landfilled by 2050. This means households should see increased options for recycling (such as compost collection) but fewer non-recyclable waste collections. It is possible that countries such as the UK will see a return of deposit schemes for drinks containers to promote the reuse of containers and PET bottle recycling (Climate Change Committee, 2020a, 2020b; Mangold and von Vacano, 2022).

Making it happen

Tax-payer funding will be used to support deep decarbonization in UK manufacturing sectors (Climate Change Committee, 2020a, 2020b). To reduce the risk of high carbon imports replacing high carbon domestic

Table 2.6: What we buy: examples of relevant policies

Area	Examples of policies and targets
UK (and EU)	Directly affecting consumers, the UK Government introduced 'Right to Repair' regulations in 2021 (based on EU legislation) with the aim of reducing waste and increasing product circularity. The regulations require manufacturers of consumer goods to make repair information and spare parts available for 10 years after purchase (Conway, 2021). Within industry a carbon levy is expected to be placed on imported iron, steel and cement, to prevent 'carbon leakage' where emissions are 'displaced to other countries' as a result of their lower/no carbon price (also present across the EU). At the time of writing this was due to be implemented by 2027 (HM Treasury, 2023).
Chile	Chile's Limiting the Generation of Disposable Products and Regulating Plastics legislation limits the distribution of single-use products (such as cutlery, straws, sachets) by food establishments. Businesses that do deliver them are required to inform consumers of the ecological impact. Legislation also regulates disposable plastic beverage bottles. Specific targets include: • ban of single use plastics in 2021 across the food industry • by 2025, at least 15 per cent of all plastic collected and recycled within Chile must be incorporated into disposable plastic bottles. That figure jumps to: 25 per cent by 2030 (Food Packaging Forum, 2021).
Korea	The Korean Eco-Label Certification System (ECS) is a legal, voluntary third-party authority certification to help consumers select eco-friendly products and identifies the product's environmental impact. This is a part of the country's broader Net Zero policy, aiming to educate the public about emissions reductions (Ministry of Environment/Korean Environment Institute, 2016).

goods, border carbon tariffs will be imposed on imports (see Table 2.6 for examples of this). Additionally, the carbon intensity of imports will reduce due to minimum standards of selected emission intense products (Climate Change Committee, 2020a, 2020b). Consumer product standards will be extended with a mandatory minimum whole-life carbon standard (Climate Change Committee, 2020a, 2020b). Companies are likely to be incentivized to produce goods that last longer (Climate Assembly UK, 2020). Product labels will be improved to provide information on how it is made, the level of recycled and critical material content, and how durable, repairable and upgradable it is (Climate Assembly UK, 2020).

Impacts

This is a broad area covering a multitude of different sectors. However, in many respects the impacts on households are relatively straightforward and relate to changes in the price and availability of products. While low carbon products are likely to see price reductions as a result of financial incentives and subsidies, the reverse is likely for carbon intensive products. Indeed, some products may essentially become luxury items based on these cost revisions due to their environmental or ecological impact (for example, coffee shops and coffee culture may move away from Arabica coffee, become more a premium good/service, or have a greater focus on spent coffee ground reuse (Nab and Maslin, 2020; Lee et al, 2022). Goods which produce large amounts of carbon in their supply chain are likely to see the largest increase in price and potentially have reduced availability.

The increases in product costs may mean that consumers are priced out of some items where they have become more expensive. On the other hand, the increase in second-hand markets, increased use of 'libraries of things' and 'repair shops' may make some products more accessible (this will be discussed further in Chapter 3).

Areas of daily life: work life

The nature of the change

As noted in Chapter 1, concerns relating to employment underpin early discussions of the 'just transition' to Net Zero and form a significant part of post-2015 global climate policy. Indeed, predicted changes to industries in relation to Net Zero policies are likely to affect the jobs of millions of people globally.

Net Zero will transform certain industries in fundamental ways while impacts on others will be less substantive. Carbon-intensive industries, sectors that are particularly difficult to decarbonize and those that will decline due to a reduced reliance on fossil fuels across society, will see a high number of jobs lost or substantially changed (BEIS, 2021b). While certain sectors along with their jobs are likely to decline, others with new opportunities will emerge (Kapetaniou and McIvor, 2020).

The UNFCCC envisages that Net Zero policies will have four primary impacts on employment: job creation, job substitution, job elimination and job transformation/redefinition (UNFCCC, 2020a). Job creation will include direct jobs (for example energy efficiency jobs), indirect jobs (jobs within changing, climate-friendly supply chains), and induced jobs (further jobs created by the renewed incomes generated via job measures) (UNFCCC, 2020a). Job substitution implies that the roles will still be needed, but may take a new form, such as moving from producing ICE cars to producing EVs (UNFCCC, 2020a). Job elimination describes the complete loss of some jobs without direct replacement, including large-scale mining, whereas job transformation/redefinition includes roles that are carried out in new ways but hold the same purpose, such as plumbers and electricians working in green capacities (UNFCCC, 2020a). The proportion of jobs requiring upskilling per industry is typically mirrored by the fraction of existing jobs that are predicted to increase in demand as a result of Net Zero. In other words, industries that see existing jobs dramatically change, typically have similar proportions of green job opportunities.

In terms of other work-related Net Zero policies, visions of the future often consider the role of flexible working. For workers who are able to work remotely, continued homeworking is likely to be encouraged to reduce travel to work (see also 'where we go', discussed previously), indeed, the Climate Change Committee has highlighted that 'climate positive' activities such as remote working, walking and cycling that emerged during the COVID-19 pandemic could be reinforced by government action.

Making it happen

As Garvey and Taylor state, there is no 'policy panacea' and policy ideas and solutions to industrial Net Zero will have to address multiple challenges, while being flexible as well as adaptable (Garvey and Taylor, 2020: 6). Sector-specific policies can be used as steering devices to lead towards both industrial decarbonization and desired action (Garvey and Taylor, 2020). Depending on the sector, levers could include pricing policies, subsidies, or regulatory frameworks and standards that must be met (Garvey and Taylor, 2020). Examples of existing policies in different sectors are given in Table 2.7. Each sector will require a different combination of 'carrots and sticks', with much of the policy related to work life specifically being developed outside of strictly environmental policies. However, as indicated in Table 2.7, there is a clear need for investment in job creation, education and (re)training.

Table 2.7: Work life: examples of relevant policies

Place	Examples of policies and targets
UK	The UK government aims to facilitate up to £100 billion of private investment by 2030 to support low carbon energy. This is expected to create job opportunities for skilled workers, including manufacture of electric vehicles (EVs), heat pumps and hydrogen boilers. Its package of policies is intended to support: • 190,000 jobs by the mid 2020s • up to 440,000 jobs across Net Zero industries in 2030, contributing to wider ambition of creating 2 million green jobs by 2030 (BEIS, 2021a)
Sweden	Sweden has committed US$15 million to a green jobs policy which provides the long-term unemployed with training and jobs in shortage green industries (Green Economy Tracker, 2024a).

(continued)

Table 2.7: Work life: examples of relevant policies (continued)

Place	Examples of policies and targets
LA/ California	Across the US there is evidence of state investment (and the leverage of private funds) to support green job creation including: • increase private sector green investment in LA by $750 million by 2025, and $2 billion by 2035 • investment of $76 billion per year in renewable energy and energy efficiency projects in California from 2021 to 2030 in order to generate an average of 418,000 jobs per year in the state (California Jobs Plan, 2021)
New Zealand	As part of its COVID-19 Response and Recovery package, the New Zealand government launched a NZ$930 million Jobs for Nature programme, aiming to create more than 20,000 jobs with direct social and environmental benefits for rural communities. The programme manages funding across multiple government agencies spanning the environment, conservation, business and employment – and by mid-2021 created more than 4,500 new jobs (Green Economy Tracker, 2024b).

Note: Table compiled by Nancy Levine as part of her Ecology and Conservation Level 3 placement.

Impacts

The Place-based Climate Action Network (PCAN) estimates that one in five UK workers, and 6.3 million jobs in total, will be affected by the transition to a Net Zero economy, with around 3 million workers requiring upskilling and around 3 million in high demand (Sudmant et al, 2021). In addition to this, changes in working patterns (such as working from home) may result in more flexibility and time for those workers, however this is also accompanied by an increase in costs for those individuals (space, heating, equipment). Note that the changes to work life described here can impact on most other aspects of the transition (discussed in more depth in Chapter 3).

A just transition to Net Zero?

In this chapter we have shown that Net Zero changes are wide reaching, intersecting, exponential, and will have an enduring impact across many aspects of everyday lives – from basic daily activities such as how we cook, through to more fundamental questions around where and how we work. In the following chapter, we return to the concept of the 'just transition' discussed in Chapter 1, and consider where, without significant policy intervention, Net Zero policies have the potential to reproduce existing inequalities, or create new ones, effectively 'leaving people behind'.

It is notable from our summary of current policy visions in this chapter, that there is no shortage of ideas as to how we can meet our international climate change commitments through policy. In this chapter, we have outlined some example policies that exist in the UK and abroad to deliver Net Zero.

These policies range from the socially progressive (such as increasing active travel) to the more economically conventional (for example, incentivizing electric vehicles). However, in many cases these are still very much 'visions' rather than realities.

To date, the most publicly visible climate action, is, arguably, the action which benefits those with the most resources. For example, we see substantial growth in ownership of electric vehicles, and in solar panel installations, mostly driven by the markets for these goods, by private sector interests, as well as by people that have the choice to pay for new technology. This is already creating a 'left behind' segment of people who must, for example, pay more for private mobility, or who do not get the benefits of cheaper solar produced electricity. This poses two key risks: first, it further entrenches the perception that climate change solutions are associated with middle class or wealthy households, and second, given that the agenda is actually leaving people behind already, it risks creates an impression that the Net Zero transition is inevitably 'unjust'.

To unpack these issues in more detail, we will explore the potential risks associated with the widespread changes to daily life described previously, and this will make up the contribution of Chapter 3. As outlined in Chapter 1, we argue that there are several reasons why households may not be able to engage with changes related to Net Zero. It is our contention that people's starting points in life – intersections of income, employment status, gender, ethnic background, age, health status, income, educational status, where they live, their housing tenure – all contribute to how they can participate in changes related to Net Zero. To give you a flavour of where Chapter 3 will take us, we consider two simple examples: highly educated wealthy homeowner 'Eleanor' working in a 'green' sector job will find it easier to engage with the Net Zero agenda compared with 'Jim' who is on a low income, renting his home and working in a 'brown' sector job. Eleanor's employment status renders her job (and need for new training) relatively secure in this context, she is able to make comparatively straightforward decisions about her household energy efficiency and is likely to be able to upgrade her home and can afford an EV. Jim, on the other hand, is more at risk of losing his job, may need to retrain as the employment market decarbonizes, has less agency over the energy efficiency of his home, and is less likely to be able buy an EV (especially one suitable for his circumstances).

It is also likely that Eleanor will benefit from the financial incentives (such as discounts and grants for home energy improvements, scrappage incentives for ICE vehicles). Conversely, Jim may be penalized as a result of not being able to do these things, finding his ICE vehicle more expensive to run and maintain as carbon taxes are levied upon it, with fewer mechanics able to keep it on the road, and may experience similar issues as his home energy system becomes more expensive to run. As such, non-participation in the Net Zero agenda has the potential to leave many people behind, and to worsen their existing circumstances.

These simple examples will be further unpacked over the course of the book. Indeed we will meet Jim again in Chapters 4 and 5. The key point here is that everyone will be affected by the Net Zero policy changes differently. Given our interest (and indeed the claimed policy interest) in the just transition, it is the risks, inequalities, and injustices that we are interested in exploring further and finding ways to rectify. In other words, we want to understand people like Jim's position, the risks they may be exposed to, and, crucially, ways to avoid harm for Jim. Our next chapter considers how best to understand these potential impacts.

3

A Just Transition?

Carolyn Snell, Lucie Middlemiss, Kelli Kennedy,
Tania Carregha, Anne Owen and Samanthi Theminimulle

Introduction

Chapter 2 introduced the changes to everyday life that are likely to be experienced as a result of Net Zero policies. It ended by profiling how these changes might impact different people differently.

This chapter provides the first of three building blocks in our discussion about the relationship between inequalities and the just transition to Net Zero. Here we explore existing evidence, drawing together what we know about present day inequalities across the six areas of life discussed in Chapter 2, and where it exists, evidence about how Net Zero policies may affect people and interact with these existing inequalities. In most cases there has been significant work within the environmental social science literature on the relationship between inequality and different areas of life, for example there is a large literature on housing, home energy and inequality. Similarly, there is a substantial amount of research on the relationship between mobility, transport and inequality. When it comes to discussions about the transition and inequality, progress is more limited. For example, there is a small but significant body of work on electric vehicles and inequalities, and also on Net Zero related changes to home energy, but very limited work on the relationship between food insecurity and transition policies. A summary of the main issues covered is presented in Table 3.1.

We next consider the six areas of life in turn, starting each section with a quotation from the people we have spoken to over the course of our research (indicated in Boxes 3.1, 3.2, 3.3, 3.4, 3.5, and 3.6). We also present the carbon impact of this area of life by income group, given its significance within any discussion of inequality, presenting carbon footprint data (generated as part of our project).[1]

Table 3.1: Existing and potential inequalities under Net Zero – summarized

Area of life	Existing inequalities	Potential inequalities under Net Zero
Where we live	Poor quality, inefficient, cramped housing (producing energy poverty). Housing stock variable across regions and by tenure type (for example, privately rented are in worse condition).	Lock in to old, increasingly expensive systems and technology; escalating digital divide: flexibility injustice.
Where we go	Affordability of private transport, and inaccessibility of public transport; lack of safe, appropriate active travel.	Lock in to old, increasingly expensive vehicles; lack of access to EV charging; EV range and charging infrastructure problematic in rural areas.
What we eat	Availability of affordable and nutritious food.	More expensive food, inaccessibility of low carbon foods.
What we do for fun	Affordability and availability of leisure.	Localizing leisure and cultural activities reducing opportunities for fun and interaction for those with reduced mobility.
What we buy	Affordability of existing products.	People with high carbon needs may have to pay more.
What we do for work	Limited employment and training options.	Unemployment in carbon intensive industries; area based decline.

Source: Reproduced from Middlemiss et al (2023)

As we have noted previously, some areas of research are significantly more advanced than others and this is reflected in the size of each section. For example, we spend more time and space on the 'where we live' and 'where we go' sections given the more developed evidence base compared to the 'what we eat' and 'what we do for fun' sections where existing work is less advanced and more disparate in nature.

Where we live

Box 3.1: Where we live: the lived experience perspective

The outside cladding is cracked and coming away. So I get a lot of damp into the house. And my loft isn't insulated ... So yeah, the outside of my house is not very good whatsoever. You can actually see inside the house where the cracks [are] coming through. I anticipate that by the time we get to winter that my house will yet again be damp so it's impossible to keep warm and everything else.

Quotation 5, Neighbourhood A, Leeds

Present day inequalities in where we live

The social justice and inequality dimensions of housing, home energy and warmth have attracted considerable attention. We know a lot about the different groups vulnerable to fuel poverty,[2] from early, relatively descriptive, research in this field. Race, gender, health status, disability, employment status, household structure and socio-economic status are all regarded as determinants of fuel poverty, and intersections of these can increase a household's vulnerability to it (Marmot Review Team, 2011; Walker and Day, 2012; Snell et al, 2018b; Berry, 2019). Starting with income, we can immediately see the unequal environmental impacts by income decile within the 'where we live' area of life in Figure 3.1. Emissions for 'where we live' account for over 40 per cent of the environmental impact of decile 1 (the poorest income group) but just over a quarter of decile 10 (the wealthiest group). This uneven distribution means that if additional costs to fund Net Zero policy are placed on items covering shelter and warmth, such as energy bills, the poorest households will pay disproportionately more (Owen and Barrett, 2020).

These issues also intersect with place, space and types of dwelling. For example, those living in poorer neighbourhoods are more likely to be

Figure 3.1: Share of total environmental impact covered by 'where we live' by equivalized income decile

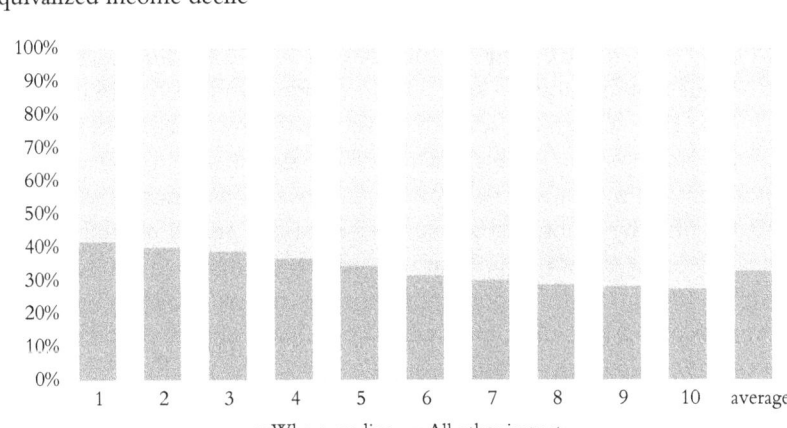

exposed to environmental problems, are more likely to experience poor quality housing and have limited investment in housing maintenance (Berry, 2019). Property type and housing sector are also important as some properties are more energy efficient and it is easier to reduce their carbon footprint compared with others (for example, in the UK, Victorian terraces with solid walls are harder and more expensive to retrofit compared with semi-detached properties from the 1980s). Housing and energy efficiency policy shapes this further, for example, in England policies have historically targeted the social rented sector, whereas the private rented sector has received less funding and has the worst energy efficiency ratings.

The Net Zero transition and future risks: where we live
Overall issues

Research in this area is relatively well developed, perhaps because the home is a place where carbon emissions savings can be made or lost, where housing quality and energy use can significantly affect quality of life, and where both energy and social policies can have harmful unintended consequences if they are not sufficiently integrated.

Substantial work has been conducted on policies that aim to reduce carbon emissions from the home. A long-standing concern within the literature is that policy action that increases home energy costs (such as through carbon levies/taxes) will lead to more widespread, deeper energy poverty (Bouzarovski and Simcock, 2017; Berry, 2019). Research also highlights issues with specific policies, Snell et al (2018a) for example, are highly critical of the way that most English home energy efficiency schemes are funded via energy bills, arguing that this is regressive, harming those on lowest incomes the most.

In general there is concern throughout existing research that low income and/or energy poor households may struggle to keep up with the changes brought about by the Net Zero transition (Gillard et al, 2017; Snell et al, 2018a; Chapman and Okushima, 2019; Powells and Fell, 2019; Johnson, 2020; Kelly et al, 2020; Calver and Simcock, 2021). Going further, Kelly et al (2020) argue that fuel poverty itself will slow down the transition to Net Zero, concluding that: 'Given the scale of transitional changes required in energy use and heating systems ... it is vital that viable national policy interventions are not derailed by generic risks of energy poverty but, rather, that policy is supported in targeting complementary solutions' (Kelly et al, 2020: 19). This latter point is very important – it was clear when we conducted the research underpinning this book that most people we spoke to were in no position to upgrade their homes, while at the same time were living in the poor quality, cold damp housing conditions described in Box 3.1.

There is also a note of warning about the unintended consequences of interventions that improve housing quality. For example, Platten et al (2020) discuss the risks of 'renoviction' and 'ecological' or 'green gentrification' – where lower income tenants are faced with increasing, and eventually unmanageable rents as a result of energy efficiency improvements.

Given the significance of domestic housing to Net Zero and the large body of existing research in this area, we now consider research on the specific changes associated with the transition (as introduced in Chapter 2).

Changes that affect the home: retrofit

As identified in Chapter 2, retrofit of poor quality, older housing is an essential part of Net Zero policy, especially in the UK given its inefficient housing compared to other similar countries. Retrofit typically entails replacing windows, improving insulation and updating heating and ventilation systems.

There are barriers to accessing retrofit measures. Retrofit is often costly, for example, at the time of writing the cost of having basic internal wall insulation in a typical English semi-detached house was £2,700 (Energy Saving Trust, 2025). For many households, especially those on low incomes, this is too expensive. While grants and loans may exist to encourage retrofit, research shows that the eligibility criteria for free interventions are often based on blunt measures (such as receipt of certain welfare benefits or living in certain postcodes), and as a result, not everyone in need is eligible (Gillard et al, 2017; Snell et al, 2018a). Indeed, many of the people we spoke to during our research told us that they were either ineligible for financial support, didn't want to get into debt by taking up the offer of a loan, or when offered a subsidy, still couldn't afford the rest of the cost of retrofit. As highlighted throughout this book, inequalities often intersect. For example, low income households who rent rather than own their home may find it harder to access retrofit given that they are likely to require landlord permission in addition to negotiating financial barriers.

There is also a small body of literature that considers why households do not take up measures available to them, even when they are free. Reasons tend to include: the burden of proof and paperwork required, physical barriers such as clearing space, concerns around disruption and mess, concerns around disruption to the energy supply, concerns about using new technology, overwhelm, and a lack of aftercare from the installer (Reames, 2016; Snell et al, 2018a; Streimikiene et al, 2020). Several ways are suggested to help overcome these issues – Reames (2016) argues that proactive, targeted, area or community-based approaches are one way of helping to overcome social and cultural barriers. Other research points to the need to normalize retrofit, for example through a 'show home', that householders can visit so that they can understand what retrofit entails (Snell et al, 2018a; Streimikiene et al, 2020). The power of social networks is also significant here – Snell et al (2018a) found that where members of a social network had already had measures installed, others were more likely to follow.

Changes that affect the home: heat pumps

There is a small amount of research that has been undertaken around some of the larger, and (at the time of writing) more radical changes to the way that we live. Chapter 2 discussed the significance of changing domestic energy systems – for example with a shift from those using natural gas to the use of heat pumps. These changes are significant, requiring substantial physical changes within the home. Research on these types of 'big' changes within the home raises risks that are not currently being considered within policy discussions. For example, in research by Calver et al (2022), despite being offered free installation of a heat pump, many tenants were reluctant to go ahead with it due to concerns about the disruption its installation might cause. Those who did go ahead experienced changes in their daily lives, and problems using the new system and associated technology.

The impact of these changes within the home should not be underestimated – Scott and Powells (2020) present some of the only justice-based research conducted on the transition to hydrogen gas. They warn that changes to the 'meanings and materialities' within the home, particularly cooking and heating, may cause 'arrhythmia' – disrupting daily lives. For example, they highlight the substantial changes in the way that households will need to think about and go about cooking food.

Changing energy systems: community energy

The rise of decentralized energy means that there is a greater role for community-based energy schemes (cooperatives, community owned companies, and so on). While a relatively new area of research, several case studies on community energy – for example, district heating and/or local generation schemes have been conducted, mostly in Europe.

There is some optimistic discussion within existing research about the potential for a 'new energy democracy' given the potential shift from big energy companies to small-scale generation (Bray and Ford, 2021). However, there are also concerns about spatial inequalities, the emerging evidence from European studies suggesting that community owned energy schemes occur more frequently in wealthy communities.

Changes that affect the home: smart home technology and demand side reduction

The increased use of smart home technology raises several issues of justice and inequality. A particular concern is the widening of the digital divide, and creation of a 'carbon literate elite' (Martiskainen et al, 2021: 778), that can engage with the technology, while those unable to use it are left to rely on old, polluting technologies. Research warns about the groups or intersections of groups that are likely to be left behind by this aspect of the transition – with older people increasingly falling behind on smart home innovations, alongside intersections of low income, disabled people, ethnic minorities and women (Martiskainen et al, 2021; Sovacool et al, 2021). Here affordable home broadband (needed to run smart homes) and IT literacy and skills are essential to ensure inclusion within the transition (Sovacool et al, 2021).

There is also a growing literature on demand side reduction/management which is often closely linked to smart home technology. This is essentially about managing demand on the electricity grid, something that will become more commonplace during the Net Zero transition given the greater emphasis placed on electricity use (Adams et al, 2021). Demand side reduction tends to require more flexibility from household energy users – something that can be achieved by directing household behaviours in several ways:

- financial incentives/penalties that incentivize energy use at a certain time of the day
- automation via in-house smart technology
- automation via external control

Demand side reduction and management measures may include financial incentives – for example, by rewarding a household for not using energy during a 'peak' period (either a set period or it a period that the supplier warns the customer about by text message). Calver and Simcock (2021) suggest that a range of infrastructural, financial, psychological and skills-based barriers may prevent vulnerable households from accessing these benefits. Demand side reduction and management measures are based on the notion of flexibility, however, the capacity to be flexible and change energy consumption and routines is highly unequal (Calver and Simcock, 2021), moreover, flexibility is not always desirable, Calver and Simcock (2021) warn, without sufficient regulation demand side reduction and management measures may lead to unhealthy patterns of energy use. Powells and Fell (2019) discuss the notion of 'flexibility justice' and 'flexibility capital', questioning the extent to which issues of justice have been considered in the shift towards flexibility. They argue that whilst some energy users can afford to pay for energy during peak periods or are not affected by reducing energy use during these periods, others – such as those with disabilities that are dependent on energy – cannot. As such, they warn about entrenching inequalities that are currently relatively minor but may be magnified by the emphasis that Net Zero transition places on flexibility.

There is also a gulf between demand side reduction and management technology and the ways in which people *actually* use energy within the home. Adams et al (2021) find that there is an assumption by modellers and those in the industry that people will be unbothered by imposed changes to their household energy practices, and a lack of recognition about the additional labour it could bring about. Johnson (2020: 7) discusses demand side reduction and management specifically in relation to gender, highlighting that at present assumptions are gender neutral, and ignore household dynamics. Moreover, she argues that smart home systems are based on existing norms, and have the potential to reinforce these. She highlights the gendered roles that still exist within (especially lower income) households, arguing that 'Trivializing the role of chore doing in analyses of smart systems is problematic'.

Control and consent is also a recurring theme within the literature, especially in reference to external control of demand side reduction and management (Birchley et al, 2017; Adams et al, 2021; Calver et al, 2022). For example, Adams et al (2021: 39) suggest that at present 'full automation without user override and intervention opportunities is considered problematic by users', linked to issues of trust in energy companies. In short, Calver and Simcock (2021) warn that 'Users will not just magically absorb new technologies into their homes and lifestyles'. Given the reliance of demand side reduction and management measures on technology, the authors warn about the risks of the digital divide becoming increasingly bound up in energy use and provision (see also Powells and Fell, 2019; Johnson, 2020).

Responding to these challenges

A way to mitigate the risks discussed earlier is through greater recognition of difference – both socio-economic and spatial – in policy development and implementation (Bouzarovski and Simcock, 2017; Robins, 2020; Savage et al, 2022). Indeed, a theme throughout the literature is the significance of local or community-based responses that both recognize local needs and account for geographic conditions. This is neatly summarized by Robins (2020: 1) in the following: 'a just transition in the housing sector has to be inclusive and place-based ... This needs to be done in the context of specific local opportunities and vulnerabilities'.

Where we go

Box 3.2: Where we go: the lived experience perspective

When you come from a deprived estate and you're living on the breadline, obviously, I feel my resistance to give up our car. If I did give up the car, it would significantly have a massive impact on our children's, basically what we can do for them. So, you know, things like being able to participate in sports club, being able to participate in after school clubs. The fact that these things aren't on your doorstep and you do need to be able to toddle about to give them life skills and opportunities. If you don't, then looking out in these deprived areas and seeing that there's nothing there on their doorstep, and you look at kids that do participate in sports clubs or, you know, any kind of extra activities and things that you can do, compared to the kids that, their parents don't drive, where they don't have that luxury of being able to go to these places, and the life opportunities.

Quotation 335, Neighbourhood C, Leeds

Present day inequalities in where we go

There is a distinctive literature on transport and social exclusion (rooted in Karen Lucas's work) alongside the more recent mobility justice literature (originating in work by Mimi Sheller and John Urry). This research identifies a range of interconnected inequalities and justice issues associated with particular groups of people, time and space, and policy and planning. Central to these debates are concerns about income and place, and how these factors shape access to goods and services. More recently, a more critical literature has begun to describe a broader range of systemic issues that underlie existing transport systems and mobility, including: 'structurally distributed class, racial, gendered and other inequalities' (Sheller, 2020: 12). Numerous other groups or characteristics have been added to this list, including age, household structure, disability, LGBTQ+ status and employment status (Lucas et al, 2019; Verlinghieri and Schwanen, 2020; Simcock et al, 2021).

There is concern across the literature about the inequalities created by the dominance of private vehicles within transport systems (Lucas and Musso, 2014; Sheller and Urry, 2016; Healy and Barry, 2017; Sheller, 2020; Haas, 2021; Huwe, 2021). The prominence of private vehicles in transport policy has led to transport systems privileging road users in terms of journey times, space and safety, where those in the largest cars are safest, and vulnerable pedestrians (for example those with visual impairments) are the most at risk (Gössling, 2016; Sheller, 2020). While car ownership has increased substantially since the 1950s across all income groups (Lucas, 2012; Lucas et al, 2019; DfT, 2021b), the greatest proportion of carless households remains in the lowest income groups and intersects with other areas of inequality. For example, Lucas et al (2019: 4) find that: 'Lowest income households have higher levels of non-car ownership, 40% still have no car access – female heads of house, children, young and older people, black and minority ethnic and disabled people are concentrated in this quintile'.

Figure 3.2: Share of total environmental impact covered by 'where we go' by equivalized income decile

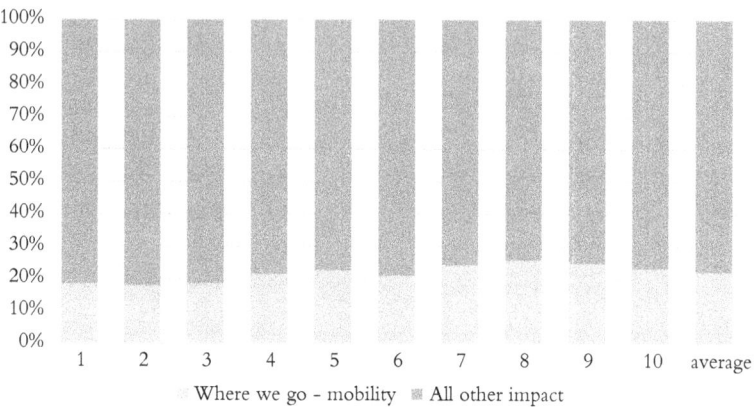

This trend of lower levels of car ownership is implicit in Figure 3.2 which shows the proportion of the total impact of the 'where we go' area of life represented by decile. The emissions for 'where we go' account for one sixth of the environmental impact of decile 1, and over a quarter of decile 8. The dominance of private transport is said to have led to a reduction in the availability, accessibility, desirability and affordability of public transport through decades of underfunding and limited public subsidies (Lucas and Musso, 2014; Gössling, 2016; Haas, 2021) with negative impacts felt most by those already experiencing social disadvantage and with the fewest transport options. Spatial factors are found to exacerbate these inequalities. For example, those on low incomes living in rural, semi urban areas or social housing estates on the urban periphery are identified as more vulnerable to 'transport poverty', where the combination of a lack of private transport, poor public transport, and limited opportunities for active transport leads to social exclusion via limited access to goods and services such as employment, purchasing of affordable food, and leisure activities (Lucas and Musso, 2014). This can lead to a situation where households are effectively 'forced' into vehicle ownership because of employment, education or other needs despite the high cost (Lucas et al, 2019). Once a low-income household owns a vehicle it will spend proportionately more income on its purchase, maintenance and running (Lucas and Pangbourne, 2014; Sovacool et al, 2019; King, 2020) and may be affected by higher tax rates associated with older, less efficient vehicles (King, 2020), leading to 'economic stress' (Mattioli et al, 2017; Lucas et al, 2019).

It should also be noted that even where accessible and appropriate public transport does exist, evidence suggests that fears around safety can create barriers to its use (Sheller, 2020). For example, Lubitow et al (2020) found that LGBTQ+ groups experienced substantial abuse and harassment on public transport, affecting future decisions about mobility. Similar experiences are had by women and people from ethnic minorities (Sheller, 2020).

Modes of active travel (such as walking or cycling) are relatively cheap or free and are often presented as healthy transport options that break away from reliance on cars. However, walking can expose people to physical dangers from vehicles, may pose broader issues of safety, be inaccessible, and lead to increased exposure to pollution (Doran et al, 2021). These impacts are unequal, typically falling along the social divisions described previously, for example, those with disabilities may be excluded from some spaces due to infrastructure (Mullen, 2021), women may be unable to use certain spaces at night due to safety concerns (Koskela and Pain, 2000), and children or those with underlying health conditions may be more harmed by exposure to air pollution (Gasana et al, 2012).

In relation to cycling, evidence suggests that there are numerous social, cultural, political and practical barriers preventing access to people of colour, people with disabilities, children, older people and women (Lucas and Musso, 2014; Sheller, 2020; Doran et al, 2021; Huwe, 2021), with cycle commuting rates especially low among these groups. Taking gender as an example, In the UK, women are half as likely to cycle as men, with physical concerns around violence and road safety, gendered roles leading to 'trip chaining' that make cycling an impractical option (Lucas and Musso, 2014; Sheller, 2020; Doran et al, 2021; Huwe, 2021) and experiences or fears of harassment and abuse preventing take up (Doran et al, 2021). The lack of diversity within cycling advocacy groups (found by Doran et al, 2021 to be dominated by white wealthy people) can mean that some people's needs are privileged over others when it comes to decision making. For example, Doran et al (2021) found that communities of colour have been ignored and sidelined within decision making and implementation processes.

The Net Zero transition and future risks: where we go

Throughout the transition literature concerns are raised about the emphasis western governments have placed on making technical changes to cars (moving from ICE to EV) to reduce carbon emissions. It is argued that rather than using the transition to address the broader structural issues within transport systems described previously, the dominance of the car has been 'locked in' and as such will reinforce existing inequalities, perpetuating mobility focused around car use, privileging those able to participate, while continuing to discriminate against those unable to do so (Gössling, 2016; Sovacool et al, 2019; Henderson, 2020; Haas, 2021). There is substantial criticism that there is not more ambition to significantly improve public and active transport (Sovacool et al, 2019a), with concerns raised about further syphoning of public funds away from public transport, and the encroachment of EV infrastructure on spaces used for active travel (Henderson, 2020). Henderson (2020: 2004) puts forward the following argument regarding the creation of a 'kinetic underclass': 'EVs might accentuate uneven mobility such that kinetic underclasses are stuck with public disinvestment in transport infrastructure and displacement from the liveable parts of cities'.

Henderson (2020) continues this argument by highlighting the risks of gentrification associated with EV infrastructure, drawing on the example of the installation of free or low-cost charging points in low-income areas of the US. These were found to have little benefit for existing residents, but instead attracted wealthy incomers, risking disruption and displacement of established communities.

Raising environmental concerns, some critics highlight the carbon intensive nature of EV manufacturing, arguing that to describe this mode of transport as low carbon is disingenuous (Henderson, 2020). Moreover, critics argue that the emphasis on private transport locks in global inequalities, with the potential for these to worsen further where natural resources in developing countries are in high demand (Sovacool and Dworkin, 2014; Sovacool et al, 2019). Environmental problems related to battery manufacture and disposal are highlighted, alongside the disposal of ICE vehicles (Sovacool and Dworkin, 2014; Sovacool et al, 2019.). The developed countries where there is demand for EVs (such as the USA, UK and Germany) rarely have the natural resources – such as Cobalt and Lithium – necessary for their manufacture. As wealthy countries seek to secure these resources, harmful effects in poorer countries are felt including environmental harm, loss of or displacement of natural resources, child labour, increased conflict, modern slavery, poor working conditions and damaging impacts on indigenous communities (Henderson, 2020; Perreault, 2020; Haas, 2021). This displacement of environmental damage is commonplace, for example, in Henderson's 2020 study, Rare Earth Element (REE) mining had been stopped in California due to its damaging environmental impact, and options in regions with less stringent environmental standards were being explored.

We now consider literature on the specific policies associated with the transition that were introduced in Chapter 2.

Promoting electric vehicle ownership

Private transport comes at substantial cost, with those in the lowest income groups least likely to own a private vehicle (or put under financial stress if they are 'forced' to own one), as well as more people with disabilities, people of colour, younger and older people, and women not having access to a car. The EV market is relatively new, and at present there is a limited second-hand market. At the time of writing in the UK the cheapest second-hand EV available on autotrader.co.uk was a 2012 Mitsubishi I-miev £5,595 compared to an ICE 1995 Ford Mondeo of £299 (2021 prices according to NationalWorld 2021). In comparison, the cheapest new EV on the market in the UK was the Skoda CitiGoe iV at £15,000, compared to the ICE Dacia Sandero from £7,995. Until EV prices reduce (either through supply and demand or government intervention through means testing or increased subsidies), it is likely that the poorest households will be unable to participate in this part of the transition (Markkanen and Anger-Kraavi, 2019; Haas, 2021), the transition will be slower (El Hachem and De Giovanni, 2019), and ownership will be dominated by those on high incomes (Sovacool et al, 2019, Office for National Statistics, 2019c). The literature warns of a 'kinetic elite' that benefits from the subsidies associated with the purchase and running of EVs; benefits from associated time savings (such as being able to drive in bus lanes in some countries); and uses EVs as a second household vehicle, sometimes specifically to take advantage of these incentives (Gössling, 2016; Sovacool et al, 2019; Henderson, 2020). Sovacool et al (2019) argue that this raises a key dilemma about how to deliver the EV transition. Policy measures that target high mileage affluent groups are likely to have a substantial impact on emission reductions, however, these are likely to be inherently unfair.

For those able to participate in the switch from ICE to EVs there are also barriers. EV technology remains in its infancy, vehicles have a relatively low range before they need to be charged (and charging can take anywhere between 30 minutes and 12 hours), in the UK, charging infrastructure is limited beyond London, and is especially limited in rural areas (Office for National Statistics, 2019a; Sovacool et al, 2019). More expensive EVs often have a longer range; however, the cheapest options, such as Skoda CitiGo tend to have a range of around 130 miles. While Sovacool et al (2019) suggest that there is appetite among lower income groups for cheaper, lower range EV, for others, range is an issue of injustice and inequality with the term 'range injustice' coined by Henderson (2020).

There are negative effects associated with non-participation in the EV roll out (and being 'locked in' to existing technology) – for example, higher costs of fuel associated with reduced fossil fuel subsidies, or the implementation of carbon taxes (Markkanen and Anger-Kraavi, 2019). Moreover, as the EV roll out continues, owners of ICE vehicles may start to face higher costs and difficulties in accessing maintenance and servicing (Simcock et al, 2021), making vehicles more expensive to run. People may have to give up their vehicle altogether, leading to the issues of exclusion raised at the start of this section (Lucas and Pangbourne, 2014; King, 2020).

Despite the criticisms outlined earlier, it is important to note that there are benefits associated with EVs and that a transition to electric mobility remains a dominant part of UK planning. Despite environmental impacts associated with EV production, there is substantial evidence to indicate significant improvements in local air quality as the number of ICE vehicles on the roads reduce (Buekers et al, 2014; Markkanen and Anger-Kraavi, 2019; Henderson, 2020).

The role of public and active transport in the transition

The transition literature regarding active travel is mixed in tone, and suggests that without considering issues of justice, improvements to active travel will serve to benefit gentrification and continue to reinforce existing inequalities (Sheller, 2020: 16; Doran et al, 2021). However, where changes are made that address existing barriers to use (for example, tackling concerns of safety, accessibility or affordability) and involve meaningful, inclusive participation, take up of active travel can be increased and broadened across groups previously unable to engage (Lucas and Pangbourne, 2014; Gössling, 2016; Doran et al, 2021). For example, Mullen (2021) argues that a just mobility system has the potential to remove barriers to walking and wheelchair use. She argues that steps should be taken to remove pedestrian severance (such as barriers often created by roads that act to prevent a pedestrian accessing their community), prioritizing pedestrians' needs over all other road users even if this means longer waiting times at traffic lights for drivers, or reduced road space. Further, she argues that the same safety measures put in place for motorists – such as gritting during the winter – should be extended to pedestrian spaces. A further example is that of reducing barriers to cycling. In terms of addressing affordability issues, Lucas and Pangbourne (2014) highlight how low-cost cycle share schemes can help to positively address this issue. Equally, Mullen (2021) and Doran et al (2021) point to infrastructure design features that can make cycling safer (in terms of dangers from other users and broader issues around crime) and more inclusive for a range of users.

Studies that consider strengthening the role of public transport within the transition identify far more positive social outcomes compared to those focused on private vehicles. This is because public transport provides options for the lowest income groups, those unable to drive (for example because of young or old age, disabilities and so on), people from ethnic minorities, and those in rural areas (Lucas and Pangbourne, 2014; Markkanen and Anger-Kraavi, 2019). Subsidization of public transport is said by Lucas and Pangbourne (2014) to have a positive impact on poor households, reducing multiple dimensions of social exclusion.

What we eat

Box 3.3: What we eat: the lived experience perspective

I don't have any money. So the money I do have I have to spend on the cheapest foods, obviously, not always the best food. I literally have to count every penny. I will go through my online bank account every few days and work out how many pounds I have left per day for the rest of them. So that you know if I think 'Oh, well I could buy…' and it might be something I really need, I might not have been able to do it because it then becomes a luxury.

Quotation 555, Neighbourhood A, Newcastle

Present day inequalities in what we eat

There is a growing interest in equality issues relating to food in the Global North, with concerns about this largely framed in terms of 'food insecurity' (see FAO, 2024 for a full explanation of this including different types of insecurity ranging from marginal, to moderate and severe). Certain groups are more vulnerable to food insecurity than others including younger people, disabled people, those with lower educational qualifications, unemployed, immigrants with no recourse to public funds, people from ethnic minorities, and households on low incomes (Tingay et al, 2003; Loopstra and Lalor, 2017; Loopstra et al, 2019; O'Connell et al, 2019). Low income is the primary driver of food insecurity, and closely linked, life-altering events such as losing employment, gaining a new member of the household, or developing a disability can plunge households into a precarious food status (Gundersen and Gruber, 2001; Sarlio-Lähteenkorva and Lahelma, 2001; McIntyre, 2003; Gundersen and Ziliak, 2014; Loopstra et al, 2016, 2019). In the UK, recent policy such as austerity and changes to the social security system, are linked to the rise in food insecurity (Dowler and Lambie-Mumford, 2015; Davis and Geiger, 2017; Loopstra et al, 2018).

Figure 3.3 shows the proportion of the total impact that the 'what we eat' area of life represents by decile. The emissions for 'what we eat' account for around one fifth of the footprint of all income deciles. Emissions associated with 'what we eat' are remarkably consistent across income deciles, unlike 'where we live' and 'where we go', discussed previously.

Food insecurity has significant cross-cutting issues with the other areas of life discussed throughout this chapter. For example, transport and mobility have known links with food access and insecurity as people travel to multiple

Figure 3.3: Share of total environmental impact covered by 'what we eat' by equivalized income decile

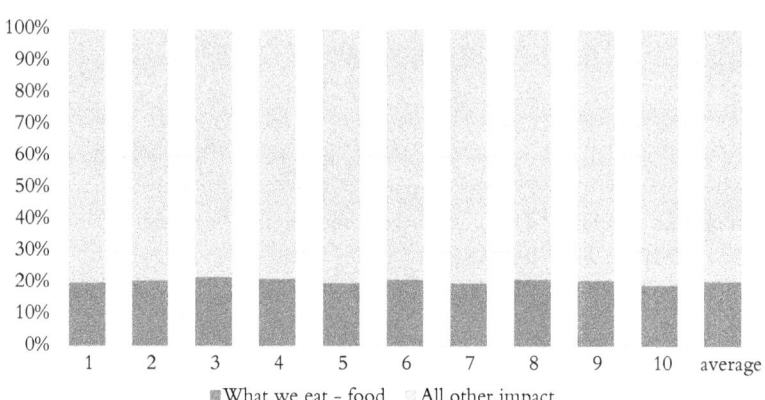

supermarkets to find the lowest price or better options (Shannon, 2016) a practice that is often dependent on private transport. For those without access to appropriate public or private transport, there is the risk of living in a 'food desert' (Guy et al, 2004) or a 'food swamp' (Minaker, 2016) where there is little or no fresh, healthy, and affordable food available. Similarly, there is a clear link to 'where we live', as those struggling to afford home energy are often found to struggle to afford to buy and cook sufficient food (see Snell et al, 2018b).

The Net Zero transition and future risks: what we eat

There is very limited research on the just transition to Net Zero and food insecurity, with the focus of transition research instead being on changes within the food supply chain, farming and agriculture. Perhaps this is not surprising given that at the point of purchase the customer has free choice over what food they buy and consume, and this is very unlikely to change compared to other policy areas. For example, high carbon food products such as red meat are unlikely to be phased out in the way petrol and diesel cars will be. At present, certainly in the UK, given that policy decisions are largely made *before* food reaches the consumer, there is limited scope for further intervention that goes beyond encouraging behavioural change.

The available research on the Net Zero–food insecurity relationship is limited and lacks nuance (especially compared to the other areas of life discussed in this review), with broad concerns expressed about the impact of Net Zero-related changes within food supply chains. Here the main concern is that Net Zero-related changes may lead to increased food prices, worsening food insecurity as a result (Fitzpatrick et al, 2018; Scott et al, 2018). Dietary change and food waste reduction are the primary ways in which members of the public can reduce their food related carbon footprint, with dietary change having the most significant impact (Garvey et al, 2021).

Dietary change

Chapter 2 highlighted how food-related Net Zero policies are likely to *encourage* a reduction in the consumption of meat and dairy products. For example, the National Food Strategy recommends a 30 per cent decrease in meat consumption as well as a 20 per cent reduction in dairy consumption by 2030 (Dimbleby, 2021). The EAT-Lancet Commission has outlined their own 'planetary health diet' standard, which advises for G20 members to reduce their red meat, refined products and sugar consumption levels while increasing intake of nuts, wholegrains, vegetables and fruits (EAT-Lancet Commission, 2021). Within the very limited literature that exists, concerns are raised about the affordability of plant-based diets and dairy alternatives, alongside concerns that a switch to these may be difficult and unappealing for many, especially those on low incomes. For example, Tobi et al (2023: 5) find that while in *theory* low carbon diets can be just as affordable as their high carbon counterparts, in *practice* low carbon diets are typically more expensive, rendering them inaccessible to low-income households (see also Reynolds et al's 2019 discussion of how to make such diets more accessible). Given this, there are warnings about the implications of leaving people behind during the transition, with the suggestion that health inequalities may be furthered deepened and entrenched between those who can easily change to a low carbon, and often healthier (Health Expert Advisory Group, 2020) diet compared to those who cannot (Tobi et al, 2023).

While the combination of low incomes, increased food prices because of changes within the supply chain, and the affordability of low carbon foods are identified as the greatest risks during the transition to Net Zero (Marmot et al, 2020; Tobi et al, 2023), they are not the only factor. As indicated previously, other factors such as fuel poverty may also prevent engagement with cooking and eating certain foods, alongside having the time and energy to prepare, cook and consume food in different ways (see our discussion on 'arrhythmia') (Tobi et al, 2023). This suggests that, enabling a shift to low carbon diets may require using a range of policy intervention that go beyond affordability (Reynolds et al, 2019; Health Expert Advisory Group, 2020; Tobi et al, 2023).

Food waste

The issue of food waste, and the just transition to Net Zero is currently not present within existing literature on the *just* transition (although there is plenty written about how it might be reduced in general terms). However, what does exist is an increased criticism of attempts to reduce food waste by redistributing food to those in poverty – seen by some as a 'win-win' situation. This increasingly popular solution to the food waste problem has received criticism for being undignified and unethical (Papargyropoulou et al, 2014; Kennedy and Snell, 2023), raising questions over its use as a policy approach.

What we do for fun

> **Box 3.4: What we do for fun: the lived experience perspective**
>
> We want to do Disneyland [in] about three or four years ... and I know that's kind of a £20,000 pounds, it's worth the commitment. And from a really selfish point of view, I'd rather spend on like, making memories with my family than switch into an electric car or a, you know, a new sort of boiler.
>
> Quotation 593, Neighbourhood B, Newcastle

Present day inequalities in what we do for fun

In approaching this through the idea of 'what we do for fun', we were particularly interested in spatial and social (in)equality in access to opportunities to have fun, and concerns around income and affordability of recreation and leisure time. Some groups have been commonly identified to be disadvantaged in fun and leisure, such as people with disabilities, and those on low incomes (Pagán, 2015; Wästerfors and Hansson, 2017). Figure 3.4 shows the proportion of the total impact that the 'what we do for fun' area of life represents by decile. The emissions for 'what we do for fun' account for under one tenth of decile 1 but around 15 per cent of decile 10. It is interesting to note that as a result, this means if additional costs to fund Net Zero policy are placed on items covering leisure, such as flights, this type of taxation would be progressive as it will affect those on the highest incomes.

This is an interesting area of life for us, because many of the inequality issues that we talk about in what follows are not obviously linked to the environment, instead they reflect the levels of access people currently have to opportunities to have fun. That might mean accessing nature, but it might also mean having a bowling alley nearby or being able to go on holiday. We raise some of these access issues in the following sections.

Leisure spaces

The UK has a mixed record with urban parks and green spaces, with access patterned by income, race and ethnicity, and disability (The Health

Figure 3.4: Share of total environmental impact covered by 'what we do for fun' by equivalized income decile

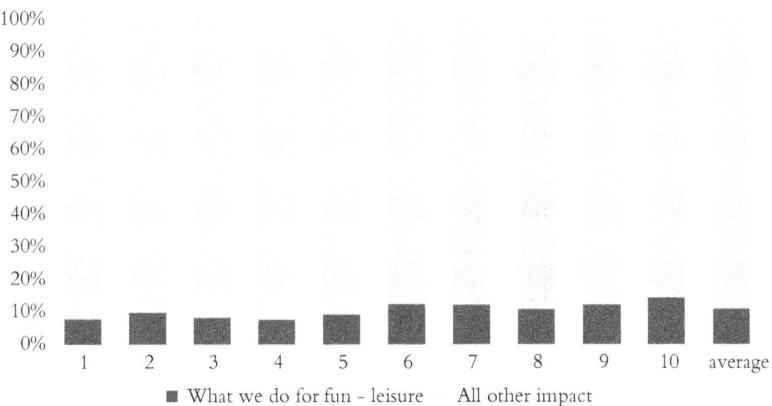

Foundation, 2024). Taking race and ethnicity as an example, there is a small but growing body of research highlighting a lack of access to good quality green space, with the Health Foundation (2024) finding that 40 per cent of Black British, Caribbean or African people live in areas with the least access to green space, compared to 13 per cent of those from a white background. This can in part be accounted for by where people live, with a higher proportion of people from ethnic minorities living in cities where there is often less good quality green space (Friends of the Earth, 2020). Further research, however, suggests that use of natural outdoor spaces beyond the doorstep (such as the rural countryside and national parks), remains a 'White activity', with people from ethnic minorities accessing these spaces at a much lower rate (Natural England, 2019).

Access is not the only issue – so too is quality. Research suggests that even where urban areas do have substantial green space, in socially deprived areas this is often of poorer quality, smaller, perceived as unsafe and prone to overcrowding. These restrictions detract from the health benefits of having green spaces (Barbosa et al, 2007; Hoffimann et al, 2017; Mears et al, 2019).

Other public spaces are also important, including community centres, pubs and cafes, and other leisure spaces. These so called 'third spaces' can offer numerous community purposes and benefits (Jeffres et al, 2009). For example, public libraries can be used for entertainment, communality, language courses, access to online spaces or forums via computer services including government websites and job applications, temporary escape from domestic life or conditions, including those experiencing homelessness (Picco, 2008; Aabø et al, 2010; Scott, 2011; Williams, 2018; Ambrose et al, 2021). The availability of third spaces is unevenly distributed, with urban and high-income neighbourhoods usually better provided for than low-income rural ones (Turman et al, 2021; see also Rhubart et al's 2022 work in the US that makes links with race and ethnicity and availability of such spaces). Funding of non-profit third spaces is critical and has been challenging in the context of austerity, COVID 19, and the cost-of-living crisis (Ambrose et al, 2021; Anderson and Knee, 2021).

Another space worthy of discussion, especially in the post pandemic world, is virtual space. This holds a specific significance for many people, offering a 'sanctuary' where people can explore aspects of their identity, interact with groups that hold similar interests or identities, and participate in discourse not restrained by circumstance or geographical boundaries (Pennington, 2018). Many groups have used social media to create online spaces and communities, with examples such as Facebook groups for migrants (Gius, 2021), online 'fandom' spaces where sexual and gender minority youth can explore their identities within a fan community context (McInroy and Craig, 2020), and foodie blog communities who share restaurant experiences and reviews (Watson et al, 2008). Distinctive inequality issues surround online communities and e-leisure, with 10 per cent of the UK population classified as 'internet non-users', primarily composed of those over 75 (Office for National Statistics, 2019a). As mentioned earlier, the 'digital divide' forms in layers, from those who do not have access, to those who do not have the capabilities and abilities to explore all the benefits of internet access and online spaces (Elena-Bucea et al, 2021). Older people can benefit from online spaces and forums (Nimrod, 2014) but often do not have access or the knowledge and skills to use the internet effectively (Hargittai et al, 2019).

Entertainment

Mirroring our earlier discussion, access to entertainment and cultural venues, such as museums, sporting arenas, heritage sites and theatres, can be less accessible or inclusive for some. Issues may arise from poor transport connections to a venue, lack of accessibility or inclusivity in venues for disabled people (Paramio Salcines et al, 2014; Renel, 2019); cost (Paramio Salcines et al, 2014), and perceived class or social exclusion (Stephenson and Hughes, 2005).

Virtual access to entertainment through streaming sites such as Netflix and Amazon Prime, can open up much previously inaccessible or unaffordable entertainment content, but this relies on relatively stable internet access and digital literacy (as discussed in previous sections) (Elena-Bucea et al, 2021). Furthermore, concern about energy costs may limit the use of digital entertainment and is known to cause conflict within households (Gallizzi, 2023).

Tourism

Tourism is a well-developed research field and has started to link with other literatures exposing the known issues of (in)equality. Issues range from the inequality of mobility, racialized boundaries and racism (Stephenson and Hughes, 2005), and affordability, with those on low incomes effectively priced out of most tourism (McCabe, 2009). Inequalities are especially stark when it comes to air travel, with UK research showing a strong relationship between flights and high income, with 20 per cent of households being responsible for 76 per cent of all flights (Mattioli et al, 2021).

The Net Zero transition and future risks: what we do for fun

Changes associated with Net Zero outlined in Chapter 2 suggest the need for (re)development of green spaces, reduced carbon intensive travel, increased emphasis on local amenities and a changing role for digital entertainment. However, ideas around leisure, fun and Net Zero remain underexplored in existing research, despite the tourism and video gaming industries having taken an interest in environmental issues for some time (Boomsma et al, 2018; Scott and Gössling, 2021). There is a particularly limited literature on issues relating to equality and justice within the Net Zero transition (especially beyond eco-tourism and aviation taxation), but our discussion of inequalities outlined previously suggests several areas of risk.

Changing mobilities and what we do for fun

As discussed in previous sections, where we go is likely to change significantly under Net Zero. Air travel will likely become more expensive as a result of carbon taxes potentially pricing out households, creating a further divide in who can holiday where and how often. Indeed, we know from Chapter 2 that policy direction in this area stresses fewer miles travelled, and more localized forms of leisure and tourism.

However, it is clear from our discussion of 'where we go' that existing infrastructure may prevent access to nearby forms of leisure and tourism, especially for those without access to a car, or who are affected by increasing carbon taxes on petrol and diesel vehicles. As we saw in Box 3.2 the lack of transport infrastructure has made our research participant dependent on a car to get to a number of social and leisure-based activities that exist beyond her community. This raises two issues: the need for greater investment in affordable, low carbon infrastructure, and the (re)development of amenities within communities.

(Re)development of amenities

The availability of community spaces and entertainment is already unevenly distributed. In the UK it has been diminished further following years of funding cuts and austerity, often affecting socially deprived communities the most (see for example UNISON's 2024 discussion around the closure of youth centres across England and Wales). Should Net Zero policies place an emphasis on localized leisure and recreation, (re)investment in these spaces will be required to prevent existing inequalities from being further entrenched.

The issue of green space mirrors these concerns – should Net Zero policies pursue the redevelopment of green spaces, without action to address existing inequalities, it is unlikely that improved access to quality spaces will be achieved equitably across communities. As such, there are questions around who will reap the benefits of green space development.

Moving online

As discussed elsewhere (for example, where we live) when considering the digitization of leisure, existing concerns about the digital divide exist and are likely to be reproduced if they are not considered in policy design. Digital cultural or leisure alternatives, such as virtual reality tours of ancient sites or museums, may be counted as options for communities to broaden their leisure options, but will not work for everyone. This may include those who struggle to utilize certain technologies due to disability, and those who cannot afford it, such as those living in supported housing where Wi-Fi is not provided. Pursuing this line of action also creates the risk of creating a two-tier system of leisure, where some communities are consigned to online leisure while others receive investment for in-person entertainment and connection, extending geographic inequalities.

What we buy

Box 3.5: What we buy: the lived experience perspective

> My home needs insulating ... I did get new double-glazed windows, about 20 years ago ... and I haven't got the money to [re-] do it. The grants are out there – I've tried to see if I could apply for them. But I'm not eligible ... so I feel like I'm banging my head against a brick wall.
>
> Quotation 535, Neighbourhood A, Newcastle
>
> Cost of living and everything has hit us all at the same time. So, if you were already struggling ... if you're already thinking 'how am I going to feed and

heat ... my kids', I'm not then replacing anything unless it comes from the charity shop. [Net Zero] is just not going to be possible.

Quotation 289, Neighbourhood A, Leeds

Present day inequalities in what we buy

Spending on goods includes items which allow people to meet their basic needs, for instance clothing and cooking materials, as well as more discretionary spending on items that people use and enjoy in everyday life. This is a rather nebulous category and covers a wide range of products that play different roles in people's lives (as well as being linked to the other areas of life covered elsewhere in this chapter). Spending on goods and services is principally related to the availability of income within households, and as such linked to poverty and spending power at different income levels.

Figure 3.5 shows the proportion of the total impact what we buy represents by decile. The emissions for this area of life account for between 11 and 15 per cent of a household's environmental impact. Spending power makes up a similar proportion of each household decile's impact, but the budgets are much larger in the higher income deciles, meaning that in real terms wealthier households have greater spending power, and the potential to cause greater environmental harm.

Throughout this section we draw on the literature on household budgeting in income poor households, to anticipate the most critical issues arising from this category. It is worth noting that in the UK, wage growth and benefit cuts resulted in stagnating average incomes during 2010–2018, with a small recovery between 2018 and 2020 (Cribb et al, 2021). Furthermore, there are regional disparities in average wages across the UK (see 'what we do for work' for further discussion of this). In addition, most households in the UK have some kind of debt, but debt distribution is skewed towards wealthier households having property debt, and poorer households having financial debt (Office for National Statistics, 2019b).

Wealth inequality (according to the GINI coefficient) has been stable in the 14 years to 2018, but there are large disparities between richest and poorest deciles (Office for National Statistics, 2019c). Further, older people are wealthier than young people, and people living in the Southeast of England are wealthier than those in the North.

Research from the Centre for Research in Social Policy and JRF paints a picture of the declining abilities of those living mainly on benefits to achieve a minimum income standard over time (tracking 2008–2021) and a shortfall in disposable income for those on tax credits or Universal Credit (Centre for Research in Social Policy, 2021; Davis et al, 2021).

Figure 3.5: Share of total environmental impact covered by 'spending power' by equivalized income decile

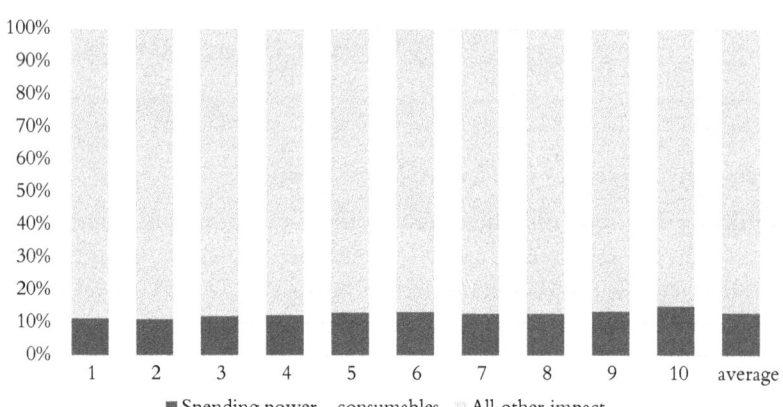

The Net Zero transition and future risks: what we buy

We would expect increased prices of some products because of carbon taxation and subsidies, and in some cases product bans. As high-carbon goods increase in price, they will become difficult and, in some cases, impossible for low-income households to afford. This could be problematic if high-carbon goods are essential to a decent quality of life. If high-carbon goods are banned outright, this could also disadvantage particular groups of people. For instance, certain types of disability can create a need for products which are environmentally damaging or high in carbon.

Chapter 2 indicated the potential for 'swap shops' and 'libraries of things' and the shift away from ownership of goods to a 'sharing economy' (Curtis and Lehner, 2019). However, there remain challenges associated with accessing such schemes, where people who live in rural areas, or who are not well networked within their community may find engaging with the sharing economy challenging (Rinne, 2018). There is also evidence that the benefits of the sharing economy are accrued by the middle classes, resulting in reinforcement of social inequalities (Törnberg, 2022).

Before we move on to discuss these issues in depth it is important to consider the links between this area of life and the others considered in this chapter. For example, the 'where we go' section considered the implications of banning or increasing taxes on ICE cars, the 'what we eat' section considered the implications of Net Zero policies driving up food prices, and the 'where we live' section discussed the cost associated with undertaking retrofit. All of these changes will have an impact on family budgets, with wider consequences for what we buy.

Low incomes and the poverty premium

Given that many people do not currently attain a minimum acceptable standard of living, the increased costs associated with goods in the Net Zero transition are concerning. In a Net Zero future we would expect households to have to manage a higher initial outlay for goods that last longer, or that are associated with increased carbon taxation, which is likely to be challenging for low-income households.

A concept of relevance here is the poverty premium: the additional costs for essential goods and services that poorer households incur (Davies et al, 2016). While many of the adverse effects of the poverty premium relate to energy and food consumption, there are broader concerns about costs of other goods, including furniture and white goods (McBride and Purcell, 2014), and home maintenance (Family Action, 2013). Given that low-income households currently struggle to afford such costs, an increase in costs under Net Zero is concerning for this demographic.

In short, any Net Zero policy that makes goods more expensive will harm those on low incomes. Where the Net Zero transition requires a household to buy new products (such as smart technology, heating systems, EVs, energy efficient technology) as described in other sections – where we live, where we go – those that cannot afford these are likely to be left behind with old technology that is increasingly taxed, expensive to run and maintain.

Need for banned products

The possibility of banning high-carbon products outright can also pose risks. Recent legislation against single use plastics (commonly referred to as the 'plastic straw ban' in the UK) has shown that such action can result in prejudice and exclusion (DEFRA, 2020). For example, some disabled people frequently need access to single use plastics such as wet wipes, straws or packaged and pre-chopped vegetables to live a decent life (Larrington-Spencer et al, 2021). Banning these items can result in people no longer being able to access life-giving products. People caring for children and older people might face similar challenges. Other waste reduction policies, such as fewer waste collections or increased cost of non-recyclable waste, may also negatively affect people who produce additional waste for health reasons.

Inequality in a sharing economy

Despite an enthusiastic response to the sharing economy[3] in academic circles, both social and environmental benefits of the sharing economy are unclear (Mont et al, 2020). Some authors raise concerns that sharing economy businesses are more concerned with making money than with sustainability objectives (Martin, 2016), with many such organizations not referring to sustainability objectives in their communications (Geissinger et al, 2019). There are concerns that the sharing economy has the potential to reinforce social inequalities (Belk, 2014; Schor and Fitzmaurice, 2015). While in principle, sharing will result in reduced use of resources and potentially increase social capital, some research suggests that people who engage in the sharing economy are middle class people with high cultural capital (Schor and Fitzmaurice, 2015; Schor, 2017), and that this can result in exclusion of people outside this category (Schor et al, 2016). Further, since many of the sharing economy platforms are digital, there is also a bias towards young people using these services. For example, in a review of the benefits of Airbnb, Fell (2021) notes that these are more likely to be accessed by younger and more highly educated people. In short, the evidence suggests that the market structure of the more business-like end of the sharing economy is least likely to benefit those with limited funds. For the more informal sharing associated with libraries of things or repair cafes, knowledge and time are needed to undertake repairs and the costs may be prohibitive, indeed it might be cheaper to replace rather than repair (Climate Assembly UK, 2020).

An additional factor worthy of consideration is that while for some shopping for second hand items is a positive, empowering experience (Palomo-Domínguez et al, 2023; Taylor et al, 2023), for others, especially in respect to clothing, there can be stigma around buying, using and wearing second-hand goods (Armstrong et al, 2015; Hur, 2020), albeit stigmas that can be overcome (Valor et al, 2022). These stigmas are well known to be classed and gendered, with working class women facing more pressure to avoid second hand (Skeggs, 1997).

There is also a spatial aspect to the sharing economy which deserves some attention. There is a tendency to focus on urban contexts in this literature (Bernardi and Diamantini, 2018), which points to an inequality associated with rural living, and the challenges of creating sharing services when people are geographically dispersed. Rural households are less likely to have easy access to libraries of things and repair cafes. Taking items for repair requires access to personal transport which is not always available in low-income neighbourhoods (Climate Assembly UK, 2020). Sharing of goods needs to be organized and incentivized and this may not work in isolated or high turn-over neighbourhoods (Climate Assembly UK, 2020), in neighbourhoods with low trust, or in communities with fewer resources.

Who pays for this?

The costs for product changes and a sharing economy are likely to be recovered through taxation in one form or another. The distributive implications of how that tax is recovered can have substantial social impacts.

In particular, if taxes are added to products, this can reduce the numbers of people buying them, but it also has a regressive effect, likely excluding low-income households from buying such products. We can see this in patterns of energy consumption under a system in which tax is applied per kwh, instead of through general taxation (Owen and Barrett, 2020).

What we do for work

> **Box 3.6: What we do for work: the lived experience perspective**
>
> When I think one of the problems will be training people in the new industries because still … certainly the building colleges are not yet really geared up to training people how to do a heat source pump, for automotive, how do you repair an electric vehicle? Do you need a mechanic, or do you need an electrician … I've seen nothing about new jobs if that makes sense and new training sessions. You know, everything's still clinging on to the olden days.
>
> Quotation 813, Neighbourhood A, Leeds

Present day inequalities in what we do for work

Labour markets have changed substantially across OECD countries over the last couple of decades, and are characterized by widening earnings inequality (IFS, 2024). The UK in particular has seen some of the largest changes since the 1980s. There are inherent inequalities within the UK's labour market including differential access to employment opportunities, job security, wages and hours worked (IFS, 2022). Additionally, substantial spatial inequalities exist within this area of life, as they do in other similar countries (see IFS 2022 for a broader discussion of this).

Taking wages as an example, average wages differ significantly in different parts of the UK, with higher wages concentrated in a handful of cities, notably London. There are significant differences in wages between North and South, as well as lower wages in many coastal and some rural areas (Overman and Xu, 2024). Places with higher average incomes also have higher rent and cost of living, offsetting gains in wages and pushing many into working poverty (Overman and Xu, 2024). Employment rates follow a similar pattern of distribution, with the highest employment rates concentrated in the South of the country (Overman and Xu, 2024). Spatial disparities in employment are not new: with spatial disparities in male employment rates observed as early as 1971. This is partly due to deindustrialization; the dramatic fall in manufacturing employment in the 1970s disproportionately affected certain places, with rates of employment in manufacturing regions falling by 5–10 per cent in only 10 years (Rice and Venables, 2021). While the example given earlier is from the UK, these patterns exist across the Global North (Gornig and Goebel, 2018; Martinus, 2018).

The Net Zero transition and future risks: what we do for work

As described in Chapter 1, early discussions about the just transition emerged among trade unions in the 1970s in the US, because of concerns about the potential for environmental policies to harm jobs (Evans and Phelan, 2016; McCauley and Heffron, 2018). While the concept is now used far more broadly (and indeed, it has been our intention within this book to broaden the term), its links to employment remain apparent, with a wealth of research conducted on the issue. Before we consider this evidence we would like to draw attention to two key points. First, it is important to highlight that understanding how a Net Zero transition will affect people's jobs and working lives has particularly strong implications for their spending power, which in turn relates to most other areas of life discussed in this chapter. If people are left behind as a result of changes to the job market, they will struggle to engage with the transition to Net Zero in all other aspects of life including housing, mobility or leisure. Second, it is important to remember that, as authors such as Rosemberg (2010) and Bosch (2023) suggest, the transition to Net Zero *does not necessitate* widespread unemployment, but does need appropriate, timely policy intervention and institutional reform.

Bearing these points in mind we now turn to existing literature on the topic. Most of the relevant literature focuses on the potential impacts of the changes to the labour market associated with Net Zero. This tends to focus on which sectors will be most affected, how this interlinks with socio-economic and spatial inequalities (while also recognizing the interaction between these). We finish the section with a brief discussion of the implications of increased homeworking – an area of literature that is quite distinct from the labour market or Net Zero literature and is driven largely by research conducted during the pandemic.

Sector based inequalities

Occupations are likely to change in the future, both in relation to the transition to Net Zero and other changes, such as technological advancement and demographic changes. This means that some jobs will become more valuable, and some will change radically or disappear including manufacturing production occupations, administrative, secretarial and some sales occupations (Bakhshi and Schneider, 2017). As the job market changes so too will the demand for workers with certain skills. Workers with skills that are less in demand, or who are unable to acquire new skills, are likely to be most at risk (UNFCCC, 2020a). Sector specific trends are evident globally and are replicated at the national level. In the UK for example, more than 30 per cent of jobs in the construction sector will need upskilling because of the transition (Sudmant et al, 2021).

The speed and success of the transition to green jobs is likely to be highly varied. For example, based on the analysis of 110 manufacturing sectors in eight countries, Fankhauser et al (2013: 4) point to three factors determining the green competitiveness of a sector: 'its speed of transitioning to green products and processes, its ability to gain and maintain market share, and a favourable starting point', suggesting that wealthier regions and industries will be better adaptable, while deprived areas run the risk of falling behind further.

It is also important to note that the focus on achieving a just transition should not only lie on jobs directly in high carbon industries. The indirect effects of the transition to Net Zero on labour markets must also be considered, for example along supply chains or due to shifts in demand, or as a knock-on effect of the decline of high-carbon jobs (Bowen and Kuralbayeva, 2015).

Spatial inequalities

There are significant risks of spatial inequalities associated with the transition to Net Zero and a number of factors are likely to worsen these inequalities. Regions that rely on a single industry (or with a lack of diversification), that lack the capacity for innovation, and with limited decision-making power are likely to face the greatest challenges (UNFCCC, 2020a). Considering these issues in the UK, the North of England and Yorkshire and the Humber (where the majority of coal and gas power stations are situated) provide a prime example of the greater challenges that some regions face. The risks facing these two regions should not be underestimated. IPPR suggests that 28,000 jobs in the coal, oil and gas industries could be lost in the north of England by 2030, and that this is an area that requires significant support and investment throughout the transition (IPPR, 2017, 2018, 2019, 2023).

However, despite the risks associated with changes in the labour market, IPPR also highlights the potential beneficial impact on the economy, suggesting the potential for 46,000 low carbon power sector jobs in Northern England by 2030 (2018, 2023). Similarly, Sudmant et al (2021) argue that: 'some of the places that most need upskilling could benefit the most from ambitious transition policies and investments'

Socio-economic inequalities

Where retraining opportunities and new green jobs are created, not everyone will have equal access to these. Where market changes result in the need for re-training, this will be harder to access for some groups, and creates risks of unemployment and economic hardship. Older people at the end of their careers, younger people on lower incomes, low-skilled workers, women, workers with caring commitments or those who are otherwise time and/or resource poor are all groups at risk of being excluded from retraining (IPPR, 2018, 2019). In addition, people working in sectors most affected by the transition, or sectors that are lagging, will be especially at risk unless the transition of their sectors is carefully facilitated (Kapetaniou and McIvor, 2020).

Under Net Zero, there will be a need to emphasize 'decent jobs' as described by the UNFCCC: jobs with adequate incomes, social protection, safe working conditions, worker's rights, and effective social dialogue (UNFCCC, 2020a). In a just transition, some occupational hazards and concerns, such as health determinants and dangers such as working on oil rigs or in coal mines, will be avoided, but other potential dangers may increase, such as exposure to toxic chemicals and substances in creating and installing solar panels or working at heights in wind farms. Without consideration for 'decent' jobs, those with limited skills or options locally could be forced into more dangerous green jobs. Further, if 'blue-collar' green jobs are not designed as decent jobs, there is a concern that there will be less industry incentive to build in quality, safety, and general protections.

Responding to changes to the labour market

Existing literature raises concerns that decarbonization policies are failing to place sufficient emphasis on the 'just' aspects of the Net Zero transition. In England in particular there are concerns that there has been insufficient forward planning to deal with future skills gaps, that existing skills, education and training systems do not have the capacity or ability to provide the (re)training that will be necessary over the next couple of decades, and that industrial strategy lacks ambition in terms of creating new green jobs (Silveira and Pritchard, 2016; IPPR, 2018, 2024). Moreover, there are concerns that these shortcomings will exacerbate the regional inequalities highlighted (IPPR, 2024). These failings are not inevitable or universal. For example, UK's Climate Change Committee (2023: 61) uses The Netherlands' management of its declining coal industry as an example of an 'orderly' (and just) transition, with retraining, re-employment, and retirement carefully managed, and with particular emphasis placed on more vulnerable employees.

Given this evidence, as Silveira and Pritchard (2016) argue, it is essential that industrial policy recognizes local and regional conditions to ensure a fairer transition. In the words of the UNFCCC:

> Two challenges that must be addressed in this context concern geographical and temporal disconnects. The low-carbon economy

may not create (sufficient numbers of) jobs in the locations where jobs are lost in the conventional economy. Likewise, green jobs creation may not happen at the same time, or at the same pace, as conventional job losses occur. To the extent possible, these disconnects need to be bridged by transition policies in order to minimise dislocation and human suffering. (UNFCCC, 2020a: 18)

Homeworking

While much of the literature focuses on job losses, skills and retraining, the impact of other changes should also be recognized. Homeworking has been regarded as a climate positive activity for some time, becoming far more common during the pandemic, and the UK's Climate Change Committee regarded the period of pandemic recovery as being an ideal time to continue this trend. However, homeworking is not suitable for all, for example, those in manual professions and 'essential workers' are typically excluded from homeworking (and miss the time and financial benefits associated with it such as reduced commuting). Equally, evidence points to risks of isolation, exclusion and mental health problems among those who are required to work from home, alongside additional costs associated with energy and internet use (Oakman et al, 2020; Griffiths et al, 2022; Stantcheva, 2022). Furthermore, access to the essential tools of homeworking – broadband for example – varies spatially, with fastest speeds in suburban and outer city areas and the lowest speeds in the inner city and villages (Broadband Commission, 2022).

Conclusion: Drawing together existing work on climate policies, Net Zero, social policy and justice

Chapters 2 and 3 represent an attempt to bring together the disparate literature covering a broad range of policy areas (such as transport, housing, infrastructure, food systems, and so on) in one place. Specifically, it is the first time that the multiple ways in which Net Zero will affect daily lives, and the intersections of current and future inequalities has been considered in this way. Moreover, we have brought together a technical literature base around the policy changes needed to reduce carbon emissions and the policy instruments most likely to achieve this, with literature on environment and climate justice, social policy, social inequalities, and social exclusion.

To understand the impacts of these changes, we have drawn on specific evidence about existing inequalities in different areas of daily life, for example, considering research on housing inequalities (most notably the energy poverty literature), and inequalities relating to transport. We then analysed research considering the risks of Net Zero related policy changes on vulnerable groups. This evidence base is relatively new, fragmented, and often highly specialized, focusing, for example, on a single policy instrument or policy change. Some literature on the impact of current and future climate mitigation policies is more developed, for example, given the origins of the 'just transition' movement it is unsurprising that there is a developed literature base in this area. Conversely, there is almost nothing written on the social impact of changes in food policy, and a relative silence on the changing nature of leisure, given its importance for people in relation to quality of life. Where literature on the impacts of climate-related policy changes is in its infancy or does not exist at all, we have drawn on concerns related to existing inequalities to highlight areas of risk.

Throughout this chapter we have commented on the links between the areas of life, making connections between, for example, where we live, where we go and what we do for work, and showing how one area can shape another. This includes, both how inequality and injustice can shape what people are able to access (such as the cost of housing shaping where people live and what kind of work they can find), and how in turn this can limit people's capacity to engage in change to mitigate climate change (for example, reducing travel is only possible within the boundaries of home and working life). The links we are making here between areas of everyday life are almost entirely new in the context of Net Zero planning and visions. Beyond an emerging literature on energy poverty and transport poverty (Simcock et al, 2021), most of the time these different areas of life are studied entirely separately, and the ensuing policy recommendations tend to be relevant to just one area of policy. This has the effect of failing to genuinely consider the full scope of change in people's lives, given how intimately linked the different areas of life are with each other. Perhaps also this means that we tend to underplay the social transformation that is envisaged under Net Zero, as we do not see the scope of it when only looking at change in relation to each area of life.

What has also become clear from both this chapter and Chapter 2 is the temporal and in many cases exponential aspect of the changes discussed. Some are already happening – for example, there has been a significant increase in the number of registered EVs in the UK, and housing retrofit has been a core part of climate friendly fuel poverty policy response for several decades. While already present, changes like these are likely to gain momentum (at least according to the policy scenarios we have reviewed). Other changes will happen in the medium term (the next 10 years), for example, gas boilers in new homes will be phased out from 2025 and sales of new ICE cars and vans will be outlawed in 2035. Other policy plans we have reviewed remain rather long term and are aspirational with less obvious plans to achieve them. For example, plans for decentralized energy systems, world class cycling networks, and the phasing out of diesel trains remain vague.

The diverse literature we have considered also draws on a range of frameworks and theoretical traditions to explain change. We pointed out in our introductory chapter, that we have deliberately read widely in order to ensure we capture the full scope of work in this interdisciplinary field. What we notice about the theoretical engagement with this field, however, is that it tends to begin with attempting to identify the injustices in current distribution of goods, work and services, political influence, or access to opportunities, rather than fully characterizing the possibility for progressive change across daily lives. In the next chapter we bring a new lens into play: social exclusion thinking, which allows a more holistic approach to understanding the risks and opportunities of Net Zero across home, care, social and work lives.

This chapter has been the first of three building blocks in our discussion of how to reconceptualize and reorient society towards a just climate future. The next chapter provides the second building block. In it we bring in a conceptual framework from social policy to build a more comprehensive approach to a just climate future. We consider what social inclusion should look like under Net Zero, showing how this cuts across the areas of life profiled here. In doing so we begin to deliver on our ambition to characterize a transition to a just climate future, which we complete in Chapter 5.

4

Rooting Net Zero in Social Thinking

Lucie Middlemiss, Carolyn Snell and Yekaterina Chzhen

Introduction

In Chapter 2 we painted a picture of a Net Zero future, based on the visions published by academics, policymakers and citizen groups. What struck us most fundamentally in our review of these visions of the future, was the magnitude of this transition as a social project. In imagining Net Zero we look towards a future in which most areas of people's everyday lives are somehow different, including home, work and caring commitments as well as social, leisure and political lives. Net Zero is a social transformation in everyday life. We also found out in Chapter 3 that change in these different areas of life presents risks associated with unjust outcomes for different types of people. In short, change is already happening, and there is already evidence that some people are hit harder than others.

We have also seen that these radical social changes are being envisaged in a context of existing social inequalities: people have different access to social, material and economic resources with which to face change, as well as varied quality of life in the present. Differences in present day experiences are poorly integrated into future visions, despite a large body of existing evidence on people's differential access to resources, and on the limitations to their agency in shaping change for themselves. And yet, opportunities to participate in Net Zero will be shaped by people's present life circumstances. In Chapter 3 we explored the existing evidence on the risks associated with the transition to Net Zero in detail, drawing on a rich literature from the environmental social sciences.

In this chapter, we bring the literature on poverty and social exclusion into the conversation, to deepen our understanding of how inequalities in the present will shape Net Zero futures. We do this principally through the concept of social exclusion, drawing on Levitas et al's (2007) landmark publication on this topic. We start by explaining why we centre social exclusion in our analysis. We then comment on the various interdisciplinary literatures associated with climate and environment foregrounded in Chapter 3, showing how a social exclusion approach is complementary to these. The bulk of the chapter consists of a picture of the present, told through the lens of social exclusion, and structured by the parts of the Bristol Social Exclusion Matrix (B-SEM). In effect, we go back to the beginning of the story: describing inequalities in the present day and explaining how these are likely to shape a Net Zero future.

Our argument, throughout this chapter, is that to build a convincing plan for a just climate future, we need to root that plan in a deep understanding of social life: of what allows people to participate in society and what does not. We find that deep understanding in the social policy literature, modifying it slightly to help us articulate more fully what a just climate future needs to aim towards. We hope that in doing so we make a useful contribution to the debates around both Net Zero and Just Transitions.

Characterizing social exclusion in relation to Net Zero

Our chosen approach builds on B-SEM, a contribution from social policy, which uses a novel and holistic characterization of social exclusion as a complex and multi-dimensional process to offer a means of monitoring social exclusion through secondary data. In doing so, B-SEM articulates social exclusion through key categories and concepts which we here reframe for the Net Zero transition. The three headline categories of *resources*, *participation* and *quality of life* form the basis for this framework. We find these especially helpful to articulate, first, how people are faring on entry into Net Zero (their access to critical resources as individuals and in community), second, the forms of participation in society that are critical to live well, and third, the quality of life outcomes that are tied to living well.

Borrowing from this approach allows us to further develop a rich existing understanding of the ways in which society shapes people's exclusion. Our work here provides an additional layer to B-SEM – understanding social exclusion in the specific context of just climate futures, which offers new and different challenges. In addition, given its origins in social policy, B-SEM gives us an opportunity to articulate risks and opportunities across the different areas of life identified in Chapters 2 and 3. For example, B-SEM encourages us to ask questions about people's ability to participate economically, which shapes their experience across all the areas of life affected by Net Zero. We also value the opportunity that B-SEM offers for us to identify what social inclusion looks like: in effect, to articulate through this social policy lens, what constitutes a 'good life'. This is a marked departure from the rather weak narrative of 'leave no-one behind' from just transition policy. We will continue this more assertive approach to social transformation in our final chapter. In the rest of this chapter, we introduce the categories and concepts from B-SEM in turn, translating each for application to the Net Zero agenda.

Resources

In B-SEM, people's access to resources are characterized in three ways:

1. access to material and economic resources
2. access to public and private services
3. access to social resources

In the following three sections we detail: first, what each of these means, second, how it relates to Net Zero, and third, what existing inequalities look like in the UK and beyond.

By characterizing people's access to resources, we articulate the key conditions of everyday life (Bondemark et al, 2021) in the present that shape people's entry into the transition. This is important because it shows us where the emphasis needs to be if we are to attempt to redress existing inequalities, and avoid replicating, reproducing and creating new ones through the transition.

Material and economic resources

Net Zero policies and interventions need to take account of inequalities in access to material and economic resources. B-SEM includes a wide range of income, wealth and financial health related aspects in this category, including income, possession of necessities, home ownership, assets, savings and debt, and subjective experience of poverty. These are all also relevant in the transition to Net Zero. As we saw in Chapters 2 and 3, under Net Zero there are expectations of change to where we live, where we work and where we go, all of which require financial resources and flexibility.

So, what are the existing inequalities that might shape people's ability to participate in Net Zero? As seen in Chapter 3, access to material and economic resources is heavily patterned, both socially and by place. This is true in the UK, but also across most wealthier nations. In the UK, the risk of falling in the bottom of the income distribution is shaped by employment status, family type, gender, age, marital status, disability and ethnicity of household head, with, for instance, people from ethnic minorities, disabled people and single parent families earning less on average (DWP, 2023). Similar patterns are observed in the European Union (Chzhen, 2017). There are also substantial regional inequalities in economic performance in the UK, with a well-known North-South divide, but additional concerns about former mining communities, outlying urban estates and seaside towns (DLUHC, 2022) as well as inequalities between devolved nations (Scotland, Wales, Northern Ireland) and with key areas of concern (such as Cornwall). This includes, for instance, lower economic output in the North East than in London (Office for National Statistics, 2018), worse employment rates in the North East than the South East (Office for National Statistics, 2020), and less access to disposable income in the North East and West Midlands, than in the South East (DWP, 2023).

As touched on in Chapter 3, research on the poverty premium has long emphasized the extra costs associated with poverty in rich countries. For example, low-income households face higher prices for energy services because they are more likely to pay bills on receipt than by direct debit, to be on a worse energy tariff, and to use prepayment meters (Corfe and Keohane, 2018). Poorer households also pay more for public transport because they cannot afford the upfront costs of season tickets (Bondemark et al, 2021), and borrow money at higher interest rates (Davies and Trend, 2020), which limits their ability to invest in energy saving upgrades.

Access to services

In the context of Net Zero, given the broad social transformation that is being described, the provision of public services is hugely important. The provision of public services under Net Zero is likely to come up against challenges associated with the current distribution of public services, and the inequality in life chances, as well as in access to such services. B-SEM describes this category as including public services, utilities, transport, private services (for example, childcare and home care), and financial services.

From the perspective of Net Zero, we see access to services, or what is called public and social infrastructure in this field, as crucially important. This includes a very wide range of infrastructures that allow people to live good lives in their place, including work, education, social and cultural lives. Given the emphasis on localization and reducing fossil-fuel using mobility in much Net Zero policy, as discussed in Chapter 2, having access to services will include the availability of low-carbon mobility (public and active transport) to get to places of work, education and fun; or the provision of those facilities and opportunities closer to home.

The presence of public services relies on public spending, in a context in which cuts in local authority funding have reduced their capacity to mend or invest (Snell et al, 2018a). These cuts have been experienced across the board, however there are still regional inequalities. For instance, in the UK, public spending, especially as related to transport and research and development, is heavily concentrated in London and the South East (Davenport and Zaranko, 2020), with 40 per cent of England's total national infrastructure funding spent on projects and programmes in Greater London (Arnold et al, 2019). Further, some of the regions with the highest levels of deprivation have consistently received the lowest levels of investment (The Young Foundation, 2019). Indeed, the most deprived communities in the North of England have faced declines in funding across the board, further exacerbating health and other inequalities (Marmot et al, 2020).

An emphasis on education and reskilling is particularly important, given that, as outlined in Chapter 2, a high proportion of current jobs are likely to change or disappear, and 'green occupations' may become more common (Bakhshi and Schneider, 2017; Climate Assembly UK, 2020; UNFCCC, 2020a; Climate Change Committee, 2021). In the UK, there are well documented and persistent inequalities in educational attainment linked with higher levels of deprivation, which may lead to unequal access to the skills and education required for the transition. For example, students from disadvantaged backgrounds are less likely to achieve the best qualifications at 16 (Ofqual, 2021), and are more likely to continue their post-16 studies via a vocational route rather than remain in the academic system (Lisauskaite et al, 2021).

Social resources

The B-SEM also identifies social resources, noting the lack of resources held by many young people leaving the care system, and the effect this has on their lives. In B-SEM this is principally characterized as links to family, friends and other supportive people, and access to social support. We would argue that these are also very important in the context of Net Zero, given work showing how social relations shapes people's experiences of accessing energy (Middlemiss et al, 2019; Ambrosio-Albala et al, 2020), and the broader literature on the ways in which social relations shape energy consumption (Hargreaves and Middlemiss, 2020; Middlemiss et al, 2024a). Hargreaves and Middlemiss offer a broad picture of the kinds of relationships that shape people's ability to make decisions associated with energy demand: including the intimate relationships with family and friends, but also institutional relationships with landlords, energy companies, energy advice agencies, tradespeople, and community energy groups (2020). Some institutional relationships represent a different kind of social resource: people who have expertise in Net Zero that they can share with others to help make change more manageable.

Environmental activists frequently have a collectivist vision of how change will come about, with a belief that grassroots groups will come together to create shared and low-carbon assets (Colding et al, 2022), raising public awareness and advocating for policy change (Bray and Ford, 2021). This vision has matured, following the recognition that community initiatives aimed at addressing the climate crisis have struggled to be inclusive and representative, with both challenges and solutions to the climate crisis viewed as an 'elite' issue (Taylor Aiken et al, 2017; Murphy et al, 2021; Webb et al, 2022). Having an active environmental movement in a place community depends on the presence or potential for a strong local network which has the skills and capacity to advocate for change. In response to the risk of excluding people, authors note that local framings could help engage people in change (Devaney et al, 2020), and that there is room to leverage the connections people have with their place to engage people more broadly (Ross et al, 2021; Webb et al, 2022).

Note that institutional relationships tend to be firmly grounded in place, and there are more or less rich networks of expertise and activism in different places. Evidence from The Young Foundation suggests that there is unequal distribution of shared community resources throughout the country, with urban areas having significantly fewer community resources than rural areas, lagging in shared resources such as energy projects or community-owned assets (Tauschinski et al, 2019). These contrasting visions of how social relations work in different kinds of communities are important in the context of Net Zero because the envisaged localization of everyday life will require strong community support in transition.

Participation

Thinking about people's ability to participate in the transition to Net Zero gives us an opportunity to close the gaps between the inequality in present day access to resources (as we have just discussed), the potential risks of the various areas of Net Zero policy outlined in Chapter 3, and the Net Zero visions for the future discussed in Chapter 2. In relation to B-SEM, participation is understood as being able to fully engage in society, through the different forms of participation explored later. Note that in an environmental context, participation is frequently used to mean either being involved in democratic processes that shape environmental policy and action, or participation in practices and choices that impact on the environment. We go beyond this narrow view, to include all forms of participation in society – following the use of participation within B-SEM. This is helpful because it allows a broader focus on what a good life in an environmentally safe future looks like: it is one where we can socialize as we wish, engage in education and meaningful work, as well as be part of a drive to reduce our impacts on the climate. The concept of participation allows us to connect the present (access to resources) and future (policy visions), revealing the barriers and opportunities for people to act.

While we draw on B-SEM definitions of participation, these do need some work to enable us to use them in the context of the Net Zero transition. Here we take each form of participation in turn, explaining how we have reshaped them for Net Zero, and commenting on inequalities for each in the UK and beyond.

Economic participation

B-SEM indicators of economic participation primarily concern paid employment (Levitas et al, 2007: 90). This is also significant under Net Zero although we discuss employment later. Instead, we articulate economic participation in Net Zero as the extent to which people can make economic decisions that allow them to change the way that they live their lives, reducing their carbon footprint, and keeping up with Net Zero related changes. Economic participation in Net Zero is therefore focused on whether households can keep up with change financially, shifting the definition of economic participation to centre consumption instead of production.

To afford the high upfront costs of new low carbon technology without government support, especially with respect to 'where we live' and 'where we go', households will need capital or affordable credit, flexibility of spending power, and the ability to take financial risks. For example: as we saw in Chapter 3, to undertake the housing upgrades suggested in Chapter 2 (where we live), people must have money to spend (either using savings or by incurring debt secured on assets or income). This is clearly easier for those with larger incomes and existing assets. People also need to be able to make changes to their homes, something known to be much easier for homeowners than renters (see Chapter 3, where we live). People's subjective experience will also shape their ability to upgrade housing: this may feel like a financially impossible decision if money is tight, and if other spending is more pressing. There are also financial implications associated with households being unable to keep up with Net Zero related changes, as we have discussed.

We know how people's spending and risk aversion is shaped by poverty (Lister, 2021). Living on inadequate budgets leads not only to everyday money worries, but also to a broader sense of powerlessness, which constrains people's ability to make decisions about the future (Lister, 2021). The psychological stress of poverty is associated with risk aversion and short-sightedness in economic decisions (Haushofer and Fehr, 2014). Taken together, this evidence suggests that those on low incomes may miss out on economic participation in Net Zero.

Social participation

B-SEM defines social participation as taking part in common social activities and having meaningful social roles (Levitas et al, 2007: 90). We take a very similar approach in defining social participation in Net Zero, with the exception that we also include cultural and leisure activities in this category. We do this because impacts on cultural and leisure activities and social life under Net Zero are shaped by similar forces: especially the need to reduce the energy used in travel, and by extension to reduce the amount that people travel in everyday life. By including social activities, social roles, culture and leisure, social participation describes many of the most valued aspects of everyday life: being able to have fun with others, fulfilling caring responsibilities, connecting with friends and family.

Reducing miles travelled in the context of Net Zero is likely to have localizing effects on many aspects of everyday life, including working life, leisure and cultural opportunities, and social contact with friends and family. As highlighted in Chapters 2 and 3, travel by air, and international travel more generally, will become less available and more expensive. Social participation in local neighbourhoods is also likely to be shaped by the increase in active travel (walking and cycling). This may have positive life impacts, as increased active travel is associated with reduced crime and more social cohesion (Aldred and Goodman, 2021). However, there is a risk of society becoming more parochial as people are less able to travel (Quilley, 2013). We can imagine that being in a minority in a neighbourhood, for example being LGBTQ+, or from a faith minority, will potentially create severance from others with similar identities (see Chapter 3, 'where we go').

The impacts of Net Zero on social participation are very rarely discussed in the literature, but hugely important, given how valued social life, family and leisure are. Inequalities in the present that will shape participation include the distribution of public space, leisure and cultural opportunities, which is highly unequal, with some neighbourhoods offering very limited opportunities for entertainment or coming together. This was made particularly apparent during COVID-19 lockdowns, when some felt trapped, and others were able to get out and enjoy local public or green spaces. Specifically, as highlighted in Chapter 3 ('what we do for fun: leisure spaces'), people from ethnic minorities are less likely to have good access to green space (Friends of the Earth, 2020), and green spaces in low-income neighbourhoods are poorer quality than in higher income areas (Barbosa et al, 2007; Mears et al, 2019). Further, some neighbourhoods are unsafe or perceived as unsafe by residents.

In a globalized society, some people are performing caring roles and connecting with family at a huge distance – across continents. The current distribution of aviation use is highly skewed towards the better off, with 20 per cent of households in the UK being responsible for 76 per cent of flights (Büchs and Mattioli, 2021; Mattioli et al, 2021). Where family and caring lives take place over a longer distance, this is likely already creating inequalities: with those on low incomes unable to see family and friends abroad as much as they would like.

Employment, education and skills

In the B-SEM framework, the domain of cultural participation refers to basic skills and educational attainment, access to education and lifelong learning, cultural leisure activities and internet access (Levitas et al, 2007: 91–2). In the context of Net Zero, we refocus this form of participation to encompass employment, education and skills, given the extensive transformation that will need to occur in this space. We included participation in cultural and leisure activities in the 'social participation' section previously.

As we saw in Chapters 2 and 3, we expect a substantial reshaping of the economy under Net Zero, with high-impact products and services giving way to lower-impact alternatives. This will result in the transformation of industrial processes, which will require different skills from workers. Some jobs will cease to exist, and people will need to retrain, building new skills for new low-carbon industries (Kapetaniou and McIvor, 2020; BEIS, 2021b). Where we work is also likely to change, with an increased emphasis on working from home for those that can (Griffiths et al, 2022). There will also be broader skills and knowledge building needed to allow people to adopt low-carbon behaviour (such as plant-based diets, use of energy efficient appliances).

In relation to education, there is an expectation that education on climate change and skills training for Net Zero will need to be provided in schools, colleges and universities (Climate Assembly UK, 2020; Climate Change Committee, 2021; Snell et al, 2023), and a recognition that people will need to be supported and equipped with the right skills for success in a Net Zero world (BEIS, 2021b). However, given that access to education and skills is socially patterned (Pfeffer, 2008), there will likely be inequality in Net Zero-related skills too. The Net Zero transition promises to increase demand for precisely the high-level technical, engineering, and scientific skills (Vona et al, 2015) that are highly unequally distributed (Xie et al, 2015).

We discussed the current inequalities in 'what we do for work' in Chapter 3, and these are the most important factors shaping people's participation in employment. These include the spatial distribution of higher paying and lower paying jobs, as well as the distribution of employment, in the UK both of these work in favour of the South of England (Overman and Xu, 2024). In some areas this is a legacy of deindustrialization, with roles associated with manufacturing dropping substantially, then never being replaced by other jobs (Rice and Venables, 2021). For instance, deindustrialization in the 1970s and 1980s has left a legacy of unemployment and 'poor work' in coalfield communities and previous industrial cities (Yang et al, 2021).

Political participation

In the B-SEM categorization, political participation includes citizenship status, enfranchisement, political participation, civic efficacy and civic participation (Levitas et al, 2007: 92). As is typical in environmental politics, visions for Net Zero put a huge amount of emphasis on engaging the public in decision-making processes and in community action and activism (Climate Change Committee, 2021). There is a sense that a successful transition to Net Zero requires public support and engagement, which can be expressed via product choice, voting and protest (Perlaviciute et al, 2021).

As we pointed out under 'social resources', there is an existing tradition of experimentation with democratic and civic structures in the environmental movement, so we have some evidence of the challenges and risks associated with these. For instance, numerous fora already attempt to shape environmental policy towards social priorities, such as formal inclusion of minority groups in governance processes, and citizens' juries (Thew et al, 2020; Ross et al, 2021). Policies for Net Zero anticipate a shift from centralized policies and approaches to local decision-making and community-focused policymaking (BEIS, 2021c; Webb et al, 2022). In addition, there is a strong perceived role for civic participation through grassroots activity, including the role of community energy and transport projects as discussed in Chapter 3. This includes local people coming together to create their own local assets, across housing, food cultivation and energy (Taylor Aiken et al, 2017; Anantharaman et al, 2019; Colding et al, 2022; Webb et al, 2022).

Being able to participate politically in Net Zero futures is not a level playing field, however. Social identity can be a catalyst or barrier to engaging with climate issues and in environmental movements (Roser-Renouf et al, 2014; Unsworth and Fielding, 2014; Fielding and Hornsey, 2016). Environmentalism is still understood as a white, middle-class, and non-disabled pursuit (Fenney Salkeld, 2016; Grossmann and Creamer, 2016; Doherty et al, 2020). Part of this sense of exclusion relates to the challenges associated with decision making around such a technical and complex topic area, with an imbalance of power associated with who knows and who does not (Cain and Moore, 2019).

Public engagement through formalized participation such as climate assemblies or citizens juries on Net Zero have to date been one-off processes (Sasse et al, 2021), which have been hampered by financial constraints and insufficient resourcing for the time and effort required to engage more vulnerable communities (Ross et al, 2021). Further, time poverty, marginalization within a community or lack of skills can impact on people's ability to take part in more communal, grassroots forms of participation, which often rely on high levels of unpaid work or volunteering, or specialist professional expertise that might not be present within the community (Webb et al, 2022).

Quality of life

In B-SEM, people's quality of life is described as a set of additional elements which shape social exclusion. These are similar to the 'resources' described earlier but slightly different in that they clearly describe unequal outcomes of processes of social exclusion. In B-SEM they are characterized as including three key elements:

1. health and wellbeing
2. living environment
3. crime and harm

In the following three sections we detail: first, what each of these means, second, how it relates to Net Zero, and third, what this tells us about both existing inequalities, but also how we might measure and conceptualize inequalities in quality of life during the Net Zero transition.

Health and wellbeing

In B-SEM, health and wellbeing are a key focus, with considerations of how people's lives are affected by ill-health across the life course. This includes recognition of both physical and mental health as key elements of social inclusion, as well as attention to disability. More wellbeing-oriented aspects include life satisfaction, personal development, self-esteem and vulnerability to stigma.

The visions for Net Zero that we discussed in Chapter 2 are largely positive about the implications for public health (Climate Change Committee, 2020a). Benefits to people's health are expected to accrue from active travel, improved access to green spaces, improved air quality from reductions in emissions from cars and heavy industry, better insulated and ventilated buildings and healthier diets (Barrett et al, 2021; Climate Change Committee, 2020a, 2020b, 2021). Better insulated buildings are expected to reduce the health effects of fuel poverty (Barrett et al, 2021), and improvements to building ventilation will reduce airborne disease spread (Barrett et al, 2021). Changes to diet are also thought to be likely to improve public health, including the reduction in calorific intake forecast by CREDS and change to omnivorous or plant-based diets (Barrett et al, 2021). On the other hand, health risks associated with climate change driven warmer weather are also noted, with exposure to heat in buildings particularly risky for older people and disabled people

(Climate Change Committee, 2021). There is also a higher risk of disease spread because of climate change (Climate Change Committee, 2021). The reduction in mobility is also anticipated to result in increased loneliness and to have detrimental mental health impacts (Climate Assembly UK, 2020).

All in all, the visions for Net Zero paint a rather positive picture of health effects, which deserves further scrutiny. As measures associated with Net Zero take effect, we would expect to see some beneficial outcomes to health inequalities, but these are also likely to be tempered by further challenges for those who are currently subject to inequalities in social determinants of health. For instance, existing health inequalities associated with exposure to air pollution, where we find that more deprived, urban and ethnic minority communities are more exposed, and more susceptible to associated health risks (Fecht et al, 2015; Walker et al, 2017), are likely to be alleviated by plans to electrify car travel and reduce mileage. On the other hand, a changing climate is thought likely to substantially increase mortality rates associated with the heat, and slightly increase mortality rates associated with the cold (Hajat et al, 2014; Gasparrini et al, 2017).

It is important to reference the strong interest in health inequalities in the UK here, with ground-breaking work by the Marmot team documenting in detail the considerably different health outcomes around the country and for different types of people (Marmot et al, 2020). For example, in the UK, regional inequalities in health have worsened in the decade since the original Marmot Review in 2010 (Marmot Review Team, 2011). People in Northern England, Northern Ireland, Scotland and Wales have a lower life expectancy and more years spent in poor health than those in London and the Southeast of England. The report paints a picture of growing inequalities, with relatively little improvement for poorer communities, women and those living in the North since 2010 (Marmot et al, 2020). This is indicative not only of health services, but of the social determinants of health, otherwise defined as the conditions where people are born, grow, live, work and age, and shaped by inequities in power, money and resources (Marmot Review Team, 2011).

There has been some attention to disabled people and their interests in the environmental studies and energy policy literature, which supports Marmot's analysis of unequal experiences associated with health (Fenney and Snell, 2011; Snell et al, 2015; Fenney Salkeld, 2016; Ivanova and Middlemiss, 2021). For instance, households with economically inactive disabled people across the EU use 10 per cent lower energy due to lower consumption of goods and services (Ivanova and Middlemiss, 2021), despite likely higher needs for energy associated with disability. Disabled people also have higher rates of fuel poverty (Snell et al, 2015). This suggests that disabled people have a lower quality of life because of health inequalities, and that they need to be paid particular attention in the transition to Net Zero.

The environmental social sciences can add to the health inequalities literature in a broad consideration of wellbeing. The 'eudaimonic' understanding of wellbeing (Brand-Correa and Steinberger, 2017), developed extensively through the LILI project (2024), provides useful input here. Eudaimonia refers to 'the enabling of humans to reach their highest potential within the context of their society' (2017: 44). To experience wellbeing, someone must be able to flourish in any social context, regardless of their personal circumstances. Given this starting point we can see how social context, or in B-SEM terminology the resources available to people, will require greater consideration in attempting to transform wellbeing. Later outputs from this project included a focus on how to produce wellbeing outcomes without using as much energy (Millward-Hopkins et al, 2020), and examinations of the distribution of wellbeing within nations (Baltruszewicz et al, 2023). This work is a helpful input in conceptualizing wellbeing for Net Zero.

Living environment

The definition of living environment under B-SEM includes: having access to a home, good quality of housing, being happy with where you live and feeling safe, and having access to open space. This is reminiscent of the areas of life in Chapters 2 and 3 that we expect to be affected under the Net Zero transition. Certainly, there is a strong connection with 'where we live', which deals with life in the home including the house and resources within it. Of course, the location of home has further effects on 'where we go', 'what we do for fun' and 'what we do for work', given the opportunities available to travel, play and work in different places. We can also make the link back to 'access to services' as a resource here. Having a good living environment will be particularly important under Net Zero, given the level of importance that the transformation of homes has in the visions of the future, and the sense that life will need to be more centred in place.

We dealt with the extensive literature on fuel poverty in Chapter 3, and there is considerable evidence and expertise in understanding the state of dwellings, and their fitness for purpose. We can see that a simple measure associated with energy efficiency (such as an Energy Performance Certificate of housing) would be a useful starting point to monitor people's quality of life. However, to get a full grasp of this we would also need to go beyond that, looking at who has access to newer technology such as air source heat pumps and solar panels, as well as how well resourced people are with leisure opportunities in their neighbourhoods, and to what extent there are job openings that allow people to work in the green economy. Thinking about the quality of people's living environment in homes and places, across the areas of life identified in Chapter 2, is a useful way of monitoring how well people are faring in the transition to Net Zero.

Avoiding harm

In B-SEM, this category is titled harm and crime, and is more oriented towards understanding crime and its impact on people's quality of life. While this is not of direct relevance to the transition to Net Zero, we feel strongly that it is useful at this point to have an emphasis on avoiding harm: whether brought about by changes in climate (through flooding, heatwaves, coastal erosion, and so on), or by policy aimed at reducing carbon emissions, which we extensively covered in Chapters 2 and 3. We refer back to the idea of a 'just transition' and the need to 'leave no-one behind' here: this means both monitoring harm caused by a changing physical environment, and by policy itself,[1] but also designing harm out by creating more equitable and inclusive policy.

The environmental social sciences have done a good job of identifying and characterizing harm through the literatures on environmental, climate and energy justice (Walker, 2012; Bouzarovski and Simcock, 2017; McCauley and Heffron, 2018; Snell, 2022), and through conceptual discussions of social and environmental harm (White, 2013; Pemberton, 2015). The value of applying the B-SEM concept of harm here, is to think more broadly across the different areas of life, about ways in which people can be excluded or further marginalized by policy. We can see the risk of unintended consequences or knock-on effects from one policy area to another. Avoiding harm suggests the need for a whole-life or 'people-centred' approach to future planning, in which we look at both the impacts of specific policy areas on inequalities and injustices (such as energy, food and transport) as well as at the impacts across people's lives from their experience of being part of a particular community, or of living in a particular place (Middlemiss et al, 2024b).

Centring social exclusion in just climate futures

Levitas et al (2007) define social exclusion as: 'a complex and multidimensional process [that] involves the lack or denial of resources, rights, goods and services, and the inability to participate in the normal relationships and activities, available to the majority of people in a society, whether in economic, social, cultural or political arenas' (2007: 25). In this book we draw on their framework – the B-SEM – as a basis for integrating poverty, inequality and injustice into thinking about environmental change, as well as a means of conceptualizing socially inclusive environmental futures.

As described in detail in this chapter, the B-SEM includes three key elements: 1. resources, 2. participation and 3. quality of life. We were drawn to this matrix because of its comprehensive approach, with these key elements particularly useful in thinking about Net Zero.

When we understand people's access to resources, both economic and social, as well as the services and infrastructure that exist in communities, we understand how the present is likely to shape the future. Starting with this awareness of present inequalities is critical in approaching Net Zero: you cannot plan for a fairer future without knowing where you are in the present. This commitment to understanding present inequalities is driven by a recognition that poverty and vulnerability are created, reproduced and maintained in the way that society is organized (Royce, 2018). This means that poverty and vulnerability are here to stay, unless we find ways of breaking those cycles of reproduction and designing it out of social organization. Net Zero is a new form of social organization that will shape both climate outcomes and people's opportunities to live decent lives. Policy for Net Zero may affect poverty by improving or worsening life circumstances, and by inhibiting or promoting people's ability to engage. Understanding people's access to resources, services and infrastructure is therefore hugely important in designing Net Zero policy for social inclusion.

We find the B-SEM characterization of participation particularly useful because it refers to people's ability to engage fully in society, whether through employment or education, or in social, political and economic life. People are understood to be thriving when they can fully participate in this variety of ways. There is a strong emphasis here on understanding and promoting agency: people's ability to choose. Bringing the B-SEM approach to Net Zero, we would argue that a good low-carbon life is one in which people can choose to participate fully in all aspects of society, while also limiting impacts on the climate. In practical terms then, being able to participate in Net Zero needs to include:

1. Having the ability to engage in specific changes in practices, technology and daily life choices, as individuals or as households, which collectively meet climate change goals. This is strongly shaped by the resources, services and infrastructure that people have access to (the first part of B-SEM).
2. Having a say in decision-making around where we are headed (the vision for Net Zero) and the best ways to get there. People need to be able to create their own pathways to Net Zero suiting a range of needs and tastes, and to argue for change that works for them.
3. Being able to live a good life, being healthy and happy, and being able to access opportunities. This links to the final B-SEM category 'quality of life'.

'Quality of life' relates to the outcomes of social exclusion, including health and wellbeing, living environment and exposure to crime and other forms of harm. The quality of life category represents the desired life outcomes that people have: feeling healthy and happy, feeling safe. We know that neither access to resources, nor the achievement of good quality of life, is distributed evenly in the population. For instance, it is widely known that health inequalities associated with ethnicity and low incomes lead to reduced life expectancy (Marmot et al, 2020). Quality of life is a category that reveals patterns, including patterns that are socially and geographically shaped. This is particularly helpful in the context of our conviction that these patterns are frequently intersectional (Crenshaw, 1991; Saatcioglu and Corus, 2014). Intersections are key in any social change, as people's differing experiences and histories will be fundamental to their ability to participate. In the context of Net Zero, we know that patterns of experience are affected by both belonging to particular social categories, and by location.

While many definitions of poverty focus on insufficient resources, the concept of social exclusion broadens the scope to include relativity, agency and dynamics (Atkinson, 1998). Social exclusion is relative because an individual or a community can only be excluded in relation to the society around them, and foregrounds agency (or the lack of it) through understanding the act of exclusion or self-exclusion. It is a dynamic process because it focuses not only on the current state but also on expectations for the future. These features are particularly useful in the context of a change process that has clear future goals associated with reduction of climate change harm, but that also looks to reshape the distribution of participation in a more 'just' future.

We should highlight at this point that drawing on B-SEM in this way is highly complementary with other approaches more common in the climate and energy space, as featured in Chapter 3. Justice, a key concept in energy, climate and environment studies, provides a backdrop to this thinking, in the sense that most of the concepts interrogate the current distribution of resources and opportunities (distributional justice), as well as people's ability to shape this distribution (procedural justice). There are particularly strong connections between justice and B-SEM's 'resources'. We also note links with a capabilities approach, frequently used in environment and energy studies, particularly in the B-SEM concept of 'participation'. These literatures emphasize understanding how and whether people can achieve a good quality of life, as well as on the importance of people having agency to shape change. The way in which Net Zero is organized and operationalized will shape the ways that people's participation is created, distributed and negotiated, as well as the distributive outcomes of change. Finally, the relatively new fields of eco-social policy and sustainable welfare in social policy have begun to articulate how social inclusion and environmental goals need to be brought together (Gough, 2015, 2022; Büchs and Koch, 2017; Bohnenberger, 2020; Büchs, 2021). This work is particularly strong at articulating a desired end point of social inclusion – linking to the B-SEM concept of 'quality of life'.

What can we learn from B-SEM?

We started working with B-SEM because we were particularly keen to integrate more social thinking into planning for just climate futures. We found the framework particularly useful because of its comprehensive approach, which helps us to go beyond the initial presentation of Net Zero through distinctive policy areas (such as housing, transport, and so on). Given that B-SEM is a social policy framework, the key concepts are social, and it assesses social inclusion across everyday life. This was particularly helpful in, for instance, emphasizing that a range of forms of participation are important for social inclusion. While some of these are familiar to environmental social scientists, and indeed to environmental policymakers, others (especially 'social participation') are largely ignored. B-SEM therefore helps us to look across social life and understand the social world on its own terms before we bring in the social transformation associated with just climate futures.

We also find that when we dig down into the three categories (resources, participation and quality of life) each has something distinctive to offer to a Net Zero perspective. 'Resources' enumerates the things that people need to fully engage in society, including the more commonly understood 'material and economic resources', but also services associated with place, and social resources linked to social relations. 'Participation' is particularly powerful because it brings in agency: by centring the question 'what can people do now', it allows us to understand better the current barriers and opportunities to action. Monitoring how the different forms of participation are working in society will be an important part of tracking the change that Net Zero brings about. 'Quality of life' helps us to articulate a wider vision of what a good life looks like: one in which people are healthy, happy, living in a good place and avoiding harm. We argue that this is a more helpful conception that the more simplistic 'leave no-one behind' mantra of the just transition. Indeed, one of the major benefits of looking at Net Zero through the B-SEM framework is that we can begin to see a more positive articulation of a 'just climate future'. We want to move beyond a future in which 'people are not left behind', and towards one in which people can lead better lives, having the resources to fully participate in society, and to achieve a good quality of life.

Introducing Jim

We finish this chapter by telling a story: the case of 'Jim' (who we first met in Chapter 2), told through the lens of a modified B-SEM for Net Zero. Jim's story outlined in Box 4.1 is a composite drawn together from the people we met over the course of our research and the ideas we have explored across this book. His story is based on the place where he lives (economically and socially deprived, with poor social and physical infrastructure), and shaped by his identity and social relations (low income, caring responsibilities, working in a brown sector job, living in rented accommodation). We tell Jim's story as a cautionary tale: to highlight how without careful policy planning, the interaction of Net Zero policy changes and Jim's existing circumstances may leave him at risk of an unjust climate future. We will return to see Jim's experience in a more positive light at the end of the book.

Box 4.1: Jim's story: the risks of transition

Jim is single, 45 years old and lives in West Yorkshire in a high rise flat managed by a housing association. He works as a car mechanic in Leeds and is on the living wage. The public transport in his area is poor and he relies on his car to get to work, to socialize, and to take shopping to his elderly mother in York 20 miles away. The area is currently reliant on fossil fuel energy and the majority of housing has low EPC ratings, and most of the rental properties in the area have not been updated. His neighbourhood has been in decline since the departure of the last major industry, and successive employers including a mass distribution warehouse and a car producer have now left the area, resulting in redundancies and loss of job opportunities. Jim's neighbourhood struggles to retain its working population and young people due to the lack of community life and jobs in the area. The local library and supermarket closed recently, and there are few opportunities to socialize in the area.

How will life change for Jim?

Jim's life is likely to change in multiple ways as a result of the transition to Net Zero. Jim will be particularly affected by the banning of 'ICE' vehicles and increased use of EVs as this is likely to both affect his job and how he gets around. Changes to home energy are also likely to affect him given where and how he lives and the current inefficiency of his home. Jim has been working in the same profession for several decades and due to working for a small, owner managed business, has had limited opportunities or experience of retraining. His employer is sceptical about the Net Zero transition and sees the government's current climate policies as a threat to his business because there is limited support for SMEs to explore green technologies or adapt their workforce.

What are the risks for Jim's participation in a Net Zero society?

Jim will struggle to afford green technology (such as an EV or energy efficient products) and his landlord may refuse to pay to retrofit his home. Ultimately this will push up Jim's cost of living as the cost of carbon intensive products becomes more expensive and more heavily taxed.

At the same time there are risks to Jim's job as it is in an industry that will be heavily affected by Net Zero policies, and without affordable and accessible re-training there are risks to his livelihood.

With limited public and active transport options, and few local opportunities, Jim's social and family life is heavily dependent on the use of his car. As his existing car becomes more expensive to run, he may struggle to continue to maintain his existing relationships and activities. The lack of community cohesion and places to socialize locally may also mean that he misses opportunities to learn informally about Net Zero policies, for example energy efficiency 'life hacks'.

The lack of community cohesion and opportunities to engage in local affairs means that Jim lacks a voice in decision making, with policies feeling like they are being 'done' to him rather than 'with' him.

A just climate future for Jim?

Jim's skills will gradually become redundant if he is not trained to work with EVs. He is unlikely to be able to afford an EV himself and if he remains dependent on his petrol car it will become increasingly expensive to run, maintain and fuel. Ultimately these additional costs will reduce his disposable income, potentially reducing his mobility and access to friends, family, leisure, shopping and employment and training opportunities. The lack of community cohesion may make it harder to have a voice in local matters such as community-based energy decisions.

5

Pathway to a Just Climate Future

Lucie Middlemiss, Carolyn Snell, Emily Morrison and Anne Owen

Introduction

We reach the end of our book, having examined current policy on Net Zero, reviewed existing evidence on the social risks associated with climate-relevant policy, and articulated a more socially progressive, inclusive vision of a just climate future. In doing so we have made some important steps forward in conceptualizing a just climate future, which we begin by summarizing here. Knowing that climate policy will have diverse, unequal and complex effects, gives us the imperative to articulate a strong claim for just climate futures. Specifically: if change is to be of value to everyone, the narrative of the future must be realistic, hopeful and inclusive. In the first part of this concluding chapter, we summarize our learning from the book so far, in a series of insights about what is socially problematic in the present, and what needs to change for a just climate future.

Our work here is inspired by Chris Shaw, who asks 'What is the most that a working-class person could hope for from a net-zero future? At present, in the vision being broadly promoted, it's the same hard work, the same exploitation, but with a heat pump instead of a gas boiler' (Chris Shaw, in Sahay, 2024).

Indeed, we argue that future visions need to move beyond a narrative of swapping one technology for another, with the same exploitation and life chances as in the present.

In the second part of the chapter, we look to offer a pathway for those working in the field, to design just climate futures with the communities they belong to. This entails taking on both climate change and inequality simultaneously and ensuring that better life outcomes are linked with reducing carbon emissions. We recognize at this point that we have taken on a momentous task in, first, addressing climate policy holistically, across people's everyday lives, and second, attempting to link climate change solutions with progressive social policy. However, like Chris Shaw, we see a strong need for such a radical approach. As we said in our introduction, Net Zero policy represents a transformation of social life, which poses numerous political risks. If we do not take this as an opportunity for a more general shift towards better lives, with better opportunities for full participation in society, we are unlikely to achieve it in any case. In our view, the only feasible climate future is a just climate future.

We finish the book by briefly discussing the policy challenges that may create barriers to a just climate future, presenting a number of recommendations for national and local governments. We conclude by revisiting 'Jim's climate future' – last seen in Chapter 4. When we met Jim, we explored the very real, creeping risks that he faced during the transition to Net Zero. His story, that reflects many of the different stories told to us during our research, allowed us to explore what 'being left behind' might look like. It also allowed a consideration of the multifaceted drivers of 'being left behind' – including the interaction of policy changes across multiple policy areas. For Jim, many different aspects of his life were likely to be affected by the Net Zero transition, often negatively, including his job, mobility, his social, family, and home life. Indeed, the future for Jim looked bleak in Chapter 4. However, we end this chapter, and indeed the book, by presenting what a different, just, future might look like for Jim, based on the recommendations we have made. We hope that this provides an inspiring conclusion, demonstrating that a just climate future is both possible and desirable.

What have we learned in writing this book?

In this book, we have drawn on empirical and theoretical inputs to paint a picture of both the challenges to social inclusion associated with current policy on Net Zero, and the opportunities for a more progressive approach in this policy area. In Chapter 2, we offered an analysis of current policy visions for Net Zero, showing how change is likely to be experienced as substantive, and to affect people across many areas of everyday life. In Chapter 3, we undertook an extensive review of the evidence for each of these areas of life, documenting the risks of Net Zero policies, in particular for people on low incomes, or from a social minority. In Chapter 4 we brought a social inclusion framework together with both the Net Zero policy visions and the literature from Chapter 3, articulating a more socially progressive vision for a just transition.

In this section we bring these inputs together and articulate some key insights about a just transition to Net Zero which we use to shape our pathway. Our insights arise from the socially deep approach to Net Zero that we have taken throughout the book, and our emphasis on the importance of existing and potentially emerging inequalities. In effect by placing people and communities at the heart of our understanding of Net Zero we come up with new insights about both the challenges of implementation in this policy area, and the opportunities for a more socially progressive approach.

Net Zero policy will have diverse, unequal and complex effects

We summarized the anticipated life changes under Net Zero policy in detail in Chapter 2 (see Table 2.1). In doing so we noted how transformative this agenda will be, and relatedly, how both the anticipated changes, and the intersections between them, need to be brought into focus. At the end of the book, taking insights from our review in Chapter 3 and our conceptual work in Chapter 4, we have two key insights around Net Zero changes in relation to the just transition.

First, Net Zero will have different impacts on people and places according to capacity, conditions, resources and assets. Impacts will be shaped by people's circumstances, by the conditions of places, and how much change is needed to meet climate targets. As such, change will differ by nation, region and local area, by rurality, and by other social factors associated with social exclusion. We have particular concerns here for people who have limited capacity to shape their Net Zero future, and we note that different people may lack capacity over different time horizons and stages of transition. Those with limited capacity, include the most deprived households, for example, but also an increasing proportion of 'newly struggling' households, after cost-of-living increases have left many with limited budget flexibility.

Second, the intersections between areas of life mean that Net Zero changes in one part of life, will affect changes in another. Much of the thinking about Net Zero is undertaken by policymakers or experts who have specific expertise in one area (such as mobility and transport). From a household perspective, this makes limited sense, as people's lives do not separate out so neatly. For example, 'where we go' is deeply connected to 'where we live' and 'where we work', which in turn shape people's ability to engage with change. Further, research on lived experiences finds that household budgets are not so clearly separated into policy areas, with flexible costs associated with energy, food and mobility being frequently interchangeable (Middlemiss and Gillard, 2015; Martiskainen et al, 2021).

Structural differences in the present will shape the future

We write this book at a particular moment in history, following 14 years of austerity in the UK, the COVID-19 crisis, and inflation associated with the cost-of-living crisis. We contend that, to date, Net Zero transition planning (as detailed in Chapter 2) has been focused on future visions rather than present realities. Building on our insights from Chapters 3 and 4, we can identify specific aspects of the present that are hugely important in shaping social inclusion, and that will be critical to address in a just transition to Net Zero. In particular here, we note four key axes of structural difference which, based on our work in this book, will be critical factors in shaping how people and places can make a just transition.

1. *Availability of income, assets and debt.* Understanding the current spatial and social distribution of income, assets and debt is critical in assessing the effects and risks of change. We know that the coming changes can involve up-front costs for households to access new technologies (such as EVs, heat pumps) and home retrofit. We also know that access to income and assets, and the presence of debt, are shaped by socio-demographic characteristics, as well as being patterned spatially. The cost-of-living crisis has strongly shaped people's disposable incomes, and these are important to take into account, given that the distribution of assets has a generational dimension, as is the importance of housing costs in shaping disposable income.
2. *Access to public and social infrastructure.* We have seen in earlier chapters how the presence of public and social infrastructure can reduce the exposure to social exclusion. Understanding how effective people's current infrastructures are, and how this might protect them in a changing future is important. The presence of a cheap-to-use, accessible and effective public transport system is a good example here, as it reduces the risk of people being priced out of mobility as the vehicle fleet is electrified, and as petrol prices likely increase. The affordable provision of childcare is a more social example, but one that is hugely important in shaping access to education and employment, which in turn might shape people's ability to engage in new green jobs under Net Zero.
3. *Strength of social networks and support.* People need good networks, both personal and institutional, to turn to in their locality to be able to access adequate support in their everyday lives. The presence of support and information in the community, through Citizens' Advice, libraries and community energy groups is likely to be important in the face of Net Zero change, providing information and support about (for example) home energy upgrades that are deemed trustworthy (see Snell et al, 2018a). It will also be important to recognize where people do not have informal support in place, and to find ways of offering this (for example, for care leavers, older people living alone).

4. *Access to decision making.* Net Zero policy does not currently reflect the diversity of people, communities and places in the UK. This is a symptom of limited access to decision making, leading to policy shaped in the image of those that design it, rather than those that experience it. There is a strong risk of increased disenfranchisement in the face of the expected social transformation under Net Zero, some of which has already been realized (Paterson et al, 2024).

Specific types of households, people and communities are at risk of exclusion

In Chapter 3 we noted how existing inequalities might interact with Net Zero related changes across different areas of everyday life, and how new risks and inequalities might be created. Drawing on the extensive and detailed literature that we reviewed in Chapter 3, we can identify the households, people and communities who are particularly at risk of worsening life conditions across Net Zero policy. This offers us insights into the types of households, people and community that are most likely to struggle in the face of the changes to come.

Households and people that are likely to face the most challenges in the transition include:

- *Households that are financially worse off.* The risks here are associated with the range of ways in which people can be financially excluded. Households at risk include those with no or low savings and high levels of debt; no or little flexibility in living costs and spending power; high economic and social dependencies (caring, parenting, time-poor due to work demands); with constraints in being able to afford upfront, or ongoing costs of home adaptations or other adjustments.
- *Households who have no power to make changes at home* to adapt to a changing climate, retrofit and changing energy use. This includes tenants and part, social or shared owners.
- *People who are long-term unemployed or underemployed*, and/or who have limited access to training, job vacancies and development opportunities for 'green' jobs.

Note that there are strong demographic patterns associated with households that are financially worse off, and households that have no power to change. Low-income households are more likely to be in rented accommodation, and in turn more likely to be female led, from an ethnic minority, and/or containing people with disabilities.

There are also specific risks facing people based in poorly served and/or poorly engaged communities. This includes:

- *Isolated or remote communities, or communities where services, amenities and/or leisure facilities are limited.* Note that rural communities are clearly a key risk here, but that communities sited in urban areas can also suffer from severance from services (see Chapter 3, 'where we go'). The particular concerns here are with relation to communities which have limited and/or expensive public transport, limited civic and social infrastructure (such as libraries, community centres and parks), and/or limited green space.
- *Communities with no room for low-carbon and community infrastructure*, including dense and high-rise housing, and communities which have limited public space for more localized amenities.
- *Disenfranchised and 'ignored' communities* which are not a political priority for investment or political engagement, and where people see no solutions to the inequities they are experiencing and feel disenfranchised from policy choices. We are particularly concerned here about communities where levels of voting and civic engagement are low, and/or there are limited democratic or community participation structures.

Note that in many ways these lists of households, people and communities at risk are not surprising. Indeed, those at risk in the face of Net Zero are frequently at risk of social exclusion more generally. The most distinctive difference here, is the importance of people having the ability to make changes for themselves (in their home, for example) to shift to a low-carbon way of life, and people feeling like they can play a role in improving their lot politically. Lacking capacity, resources, and power to make changes in everyday living, and exclusion from political decision-making, become the critical exclusions within transition to Net Zero.

Mechanisms of exclusion cut across areas of life

Building on the findings of early chapters, we are also able to characterize how people are excluded, identifying several mechanisms that shape people's ability to cope with change. We note here that these often cut across the different areas of life that we identified in Chapter 2. In summary, people are excluded from engaging in Net Zero related changes:

- *When upfront costs of change are prohibitive:* with people being left behind when they cannot adopt change early. This includes the cost of new technology, but also the costs of education and retraining. Clearly those with less financial flexibility are less able to act early and will likely lose out as a result.

- *When people cannot afford to make changes due to the costs of other things:* for example, as a result of the poverty premium and rising cost of living leaving insufficient funds for Net Zero related activities, or due to the cost of upgrading housing which was in worse condition to start with.
- *When people do not have the power to make a change*: including both when people are disempowered through fear, because change is just not an option, or because someone else has decision-making power. This would include, for example, people not being able to retrofit rented homes, being unable to work from home, or not being equipped to engage in political change processes.
- *When people become trapped where they live* due to the cost of travel, or due to inadequate accessibility of transport. This might result in people being unable to access work and educational opportunities, being frustrated or oppressed in an insular community, struggling to fulfil caring obligations at a distance or being poorly served in their community.
- *When people do not see benefits to themselves or their loved ones in the Net Zero agenda.* This is also linked to feelings of disenfranchisement, and people not having the agency to shape how changes are implemented in their home and community.

What is a just climate future?

The arguments around the need for a low-carbon future are well rehearsed, and we will not dwell on the need to reduce emissions here. Instead, we take a closer look at what a specifically *just climate future* would look like, inspired by our earlier chapters. We move on from current thinking in two key ways.

First, future visions that we profiled in Chapter 2 are highly consistent with each other (despite coming from a range of sources), painting a picture of a world in which we live in renovated, energy efficient houses with renewable heating and cooling, we travel less, eat less meat, access public services locally, work locally for low-carbon employers and enjoy leisure time with less travel. However, these visions are strongly future oriented, with little recognition of how change will affect diverse communities and people in the unequal present. To ensure that a transition brings improved public health, reduces poverty, increases wellbeing and brings neighbourhoods together, as promised in some of these visions, a just climate future must be more socially and historically grounded. What we mean by this is that current and past conditions will shape the future and must be thoroughly integrated into envisioning it. This suggests that a just climate future requires an agenda of social inclusion to be integrated at the heart of climate policy. Climate futures can only be just if we set out to plan them that way.

Second, and as we articulated in Chapter 4, we draw on inputs from the social inclusion literature to move from a just transition that 'leaves no-one behind' to a positive articulation of a socially inclusive climate future: a future that actively enables better lives, rather than reproducing current inequalities. To do that we build on our extensive documentation of how people are being left behind in Chapter 3, and our more progressive articulation of what socially inclusive climate policy would look like in Chapter 4.

Before we do so, we should note that given our geographic location in the UK, we have largely focused on Net Zero policy in the UK in this book, and on the differences between experiences within our nation. It is hugely important, however, that a just climate future genuinely reduces emissions from richer countries (including the UK) to mitigate the impact that human caused emissions are having globally. This is an important part of the 'just' future in a more international sense: as a nation we have historically emitted more than our fair share, and shaped people's experiences in other nations as a result.

So what does a just climate future look like? While different people and places will have different ideas about just climate futures, they do need to fulfil some key criteria. Simply put, a just climate future must be one in which people can live a good life within planetary boundaries. A good life, drawing on B-SEM, is a life in which people have the opportunity both to fully participate in society, and in doing so to achieve a good quality of life. Therefore, in a just climate future, people should have the freedom to make economic decisions for the good of the climate, to have access to a rich social life, to be free to engage in education and meaningful work, and to politically shape the direction of Net Zero. In a just climate future, people should be also able to achieve the quality of life outcomes articulated in B-SEM: including health and wellbeing, feeling safe and being happy where they live.

Our pathway to a just climate future

Our pathway is intended to give people active in this field, whether as researchers, policymakers or practitioners, a practical way of thinking through the social risks of climate policy, and building towards a just climate future. We hope this will be useful for those attempting to plan just climate futures. This might include local authorities focused on addressing challenges in particular places, or people advocating for specific social groups (such as disability advocates) looking to think through the inclusion challenges of Net Zero policy.

We anticipate that you might want to use each part of the process to think about a specific group of people and/or a particular place: starting by understanding their current situation, the anticipated changes to meet climate targets, how these might create risks which prevent a just climate future coming to fruition, and then working out how to strategically mitigate these risks. We use the word 'community' throughout to capture these combined interests, leaning into its flexibility in describing communities of place or of interest and identity. Table 5.1 summarizes this pathway.

Table 5.1: Key steps towards a just climate future: in summary

Steps	Actions	Further information
Step 1: Understand the challenge by mapping out community and household risks	☑ *Consider how Net Zero changes affect your community by asking:* How do the characteristics of your community shape the risks of change under Net Zero? How do changes in one area of life overlap for other areas in your community?	Areas of life expected to change: Where we live Where we go What we eat What we do for fun What we spend our money on What we do for work
	☑ *Consider who is specifically at risk of exclusion by asking:* What kinds of people are likely to be more negatively affected by specific policies or combinations of policies?	People and communities likely to be negatively affected: • households that are financially worse off • households who have no power to make changes at home • people who are long-term unemployed or underemployed • isolated or remote communities, or communities where services, amenities and/or leisure facilities are limited • communities with no room for low-carbon and community infrastructure • disenfranchised communities
Step 2: Build a vision for just climate futures in your community	☑ *Build your vision using the following criteria:* • Can people afford a good life, including being able to make economic decisions for the good of the climate? • Do people have access to a rich social life? • Can people engage in education and meaningful work? • Are people able to shape the direction of Net Zero politically? • Are people protected against new or rising disadvantage, marginalization and deprivation? • Does climate policy strive for more equal opportunities and empowered lives?	
Step 3: Plan for just climate futures in your community	☑ *Embed the following strategic principles into policymaking and implementation:* 1. Just climate futures recognize that change starts in the present, and change should be shaped in communities, according to local need and priorities. 2. Just climate futures address change holistically, recognizing the need for joined up action across areas of life. 3. Just climate futures put positive social transformation at the heart of low-carbon change. ☑ *Design for inclusion and design for extremes* • identify who is able to act, and reduce exclusion for others • determine transition pathways for household profiles • assess affordability of change • take the risk out of change, especially for those that are excluded	

Step 1: Understand the challenge of just climate futures in your community
How will Net Zero changes affect your community?

We hope that this book will help you think about how Net Zero changes will affect your community in a number of ways. First, our articulation of the six areas of life likely to be shaped by Net Zero policy (discussed across Chapters 2 and 3) is a useful starting point.

To address just climate futures, we advise using these six areas of life to think through:

1. How do the characteristics of your community shape the risks of change under Net Zero?
2. How do changes in one area of life overlap with other areas of life in your community?

As part of undertaking this initial assessment of how Net Zero policy will shape your community, it is also useful to refer to our articulation of how structural differences in the present will enable or prevent people and places from engaging in change. This offers an opportunity to consider the availability of income, assets and debt; access to public and social infrastructure; and strength of social networks and social support in your community. Some suggestions of data resources available to undertake this work are offered in Box 5.1.

Box 5.1: Understanding how Net Zero will affect your community

There are several existing data resources that can help to build a picture of how Net Zero policy might affect your community. To better understand the availability of income, assets and debt, the Index of Multiple Deprivation is helpful in communities of place (Consumer Data Research Centre, 2024), specifically under the category of 'income'. The Living Cost and Food Survey (ONS, 2025) is an annual survey of 6,000 representative UK households. The survey collects data on all household expenditure by consumption category; demographic and lifestyle data on who is completing the survey and detailed income data from employment, benefits and assets. This data could be used to understand the disposable incomes and debts of different household types.

A range of tools exist to understand access to public and social infrastructure, including the Transport Related Social Exclusion tool (Transport for the North, 2023) and the Index of Multiple Deprivation's 'geographical barriers' category which assesses how challenging it is for households to reach key services (Consumer Data Research Centre, 2024).

People's access to social networks and social support can be captured through measures of social capital and community assets from The Young Foundation (Tauschinski et al, 2019).

Who is specifically at risk of exclusion?

Building on our insights about people, households and communities at higher risk, we suggest you move on to thinking about who in particular is at risk in your community. The people we want to identify here are those least likely to engage with policy changes and/or most likely to be negatively impacted by them. An indication of the types of people and communities affected (based on the ideas presented across this book) was outlined earlier in this chapter where we identified specific types of households, people and communities at risk of exclusion.

As part of this process it is important to think about:

- What kinds of people are likely to be more negatively affected by specific policies?
- Are there types of people who will be particularly affected by combinations of policies?
- What types of profiles can we identify and what specific transition pathways will they need?

To answer the first and third question, we can draw on existing data about deprivation, as profiled in Box 5.1, and find ways of disaggregating this by different communities and populations as explained in Box 5.2. Throughout this process it is important to think about the collective effect of policy as in our second question here. For example, if a shift to greener employment is taking effect in a community, we need to pay attention to the capacity of that community to travel to new employment, including the affordability of travel options and the presence of public transport infrastructure.

Box 5.2: Disaggregating data to identify at risk populations

Certain types of people are likely to be disproportionately impacted by specific Net Zero policies. We may want to identify who they are, where they are and what the effect of the impact might be for these groups compared to others. For example, funding climate policy through levies raised on home energy bills will disproportionately impact those who spend a greater portion of their disposable income on energy.

To find the types of people most affected, the Living Cost and Food Survey can be used to compare energy costs to disposable income and characterize these types of households. For example, Owen and Barrett (2020) find that 'women of retirement age living alone and households who have never worked or are long term unemployed contribute above average proportions of their income' towards climate policy.

To identify the parts of the country most at risk, the UK Census can be used to find which neighbourhoods in the UK contain the greatest concentrations of these types of people.

Step 2: Build a vision for just climate futures in your community

Some key insights from our work include the recognition that we need to build different visions for people, households and communities with different starting points, and that a just climate future will involve people having the opportunity to live a good life within planetary boundaries. We described a good life in Chapter 4 using the quality-of-life outcomes from B-SEM: including good health and wellbeing, feeling safe, and being happy where we live. Based on what we have presented in this book we would recommend that a vision for a just climate future should be designed to address the following questions:

- Are people protected against new or rising disadvantage, marginalization and deprivation?
- Does climate policy strive for more equal opportunities and empowered lives?
- Can people afford a good life, including being able to make economic decisions for the good of the climate?
- Do people have access to a rich social life in their community?
- Can people engage in education and meaningful low carbon work?
- Are people able to shape the direction of Net Zero politically?

The next step is therefore to reflect collectively on:

- What needs to change to improve lives and to reduce inequalities?
- How can we achieve that change within planetary boundaries?

A collectively crafted vision of the future is likely to be challenging to produce, resulting in disagreement and contention. Given that to date climate futures have been presented as rather homogeneous, we think it is particularly important to reintroduce local politics into future visions. We also anticipate that just climate futures in one location will look different from futures in another, due to the varying make up and influence of heritage, identity, community composition and political leadership.

Step 3: Plan for just climate futures in your community
Strategic approach

The insights from this book allow us to build a set of strategic principles to guide decision making. These have implications for how just climate futures are planned within communities.

- Just climate futures recognize that change starts in the present, and change should be shaped in communities, according to local need and priorities.

This implies the need to devolve decision making locally, and to support participatory processes to engage people in decision making on matters that concern them.
- Just climate futures address change holistically, recognizing the need for joined up action across areas of life. This suggests the need to bridge policy silos, bringing discussions of just climate futures into all areas of social and public policy.
- Just climate futures put positive social transformation at the heart of low-carbon change. Ensuring that climate futures are just means making a real commitment to prioritizing social concerns in the introduction of climate policy.

Designing inclusive actions

When designing actions for just climate futures, we advise thinking through the various policy and practice changes discussed in detail in Chapter 2 and approaching them in a way that prioritizes *just* climate futures. The emphasis here is on ensuring that the most important actions for your community happen as early as possible, and that they are implemented in a way which increases people's ability to live a good life. Building from our strategic principles, and the mechanisms of exclusion that we identified earlier, we can offer more detailed guidance for designing actions towards just climate futures. Note that we are not specifying *what* needs to be done here, rather *how* it needs to be done: how the social transformation potential of climate futures can be realized.

To that end, actions for just climate futures should:

- Identify who can act, and reduce exclusion for others, based on specific person-centred profiles. It is important to note who takes up incentives and who has access to new technology, and to put in place measures to reduce barriers to engagement for those that cannot participate in these ways.
- Determine transition pathways for household profiles. Start developing pathways from the household outwards, not from individual policy areas, identifying where action is necessary and where it is interdependent with other policy areas.
- Assess affordability of change: given some aspects of Net Zero require upfront investment, or expenses that are outside of many people's budget, monitoring the affordability of change, including assessing who can and cannot afford change, is important.
- Take the risk out of change, especially for those that are excluded: people who are at a disadvantage are less likely to take risks, and any action for a just climate future must reduce risk. This includes, for instance, dealing with the split incentive associated with retrofitting private rented

accommodation, and mitigating past trust barriers through working with trusted intermediaries, to ensure that people can engage politically in Net Zero, as just two examples.

Policy change to support just climate futures

Policy risks in the present

We started this book warning about existing gaps in knowledge (see Chapter 1 'Towards just climate futures: gaps in current thinking'). We highlighted the narrow way in which the transition to Net Zero has been discussed within policy debates (in the UK, and developed countries more generally), with an emphasis on jobs and related area-based decline (perhaps reflecting the trade union origins of the just transition narrative). We also highlighted the lack of policy emphasis on the 'just' aspects of the transition to Net Zero. These limitations reflect the failure to draw together Net Zero policy debates with those linked to social and public policy. While we hope that our book has brought the interdependence between these policy areas and academic disciplines to the fore (most notably in Chapters 4 and 5), we contend that without a shift in the way that the transition to Net Zero is understood and characterized within policy debates, there are risks that it will further entrench existing divisions and inequalities.

We note here a number of specific risks to designing and implementing a just climate future. Firstly, we consider the siloed thinking and language within public policy space problematic (Froy and Giguère, 2010) Taking home energy as an example: there are substantial Net Zero activities in this area across developed countries (as shown in Chapters 2 and 3). However, policymaking and implementation is often technical rather than person focused, rarely considers the overall impact and interaction of multiple changes within the home (for example the combination of installing a heat pump and a demand side management system), and how this might interact with other areas of life, for example working from home, EV charging, or cooking. Secondly, and closely related, budgets are also drawn up in a siloed way, limiting innovation, and limiting the joined up thinking we have advocated for earlier. While in the UK there has been some innovation within the Net Zero policy space, for example the Department responsible for Net Zero working to identify buy-in from other Departments (House of Commons Committee of Public Accounts, 2024), more joined up thinking is needed.

Thirdly, the UK (alongside many other countries) has experienced substantial cuts to its public sector through years of austerity, the COVID-19 pandemic, and cost of living crisis. At the time of writing many more households than ever were struggling with increased energy, food, transport, and housing costs (Snell et al, 2024; as apparent in the examples from our research presented across this book). Given our argument that the transition to Net Zero should address social inequalities and exclusion, it is likely that substantial additional funds and investment will be required. This includes funds in the private sector to finance less risky aspects of the transition, for those that can afford to pay part of the costs. It also includes government funds for those facing challenges in transition, and for those unable to borrow or pay. Without sufficient funding to meet people 'where they are', it is likely that the transition will be uneven, increasing the risk of leaving people behind. As such, a just climate future requires significant, perhaps radical vision.

Policy change needed to support local action

So far, we have argued that climate and Net Zero policy needs to be strongly shaped by concerns of social inclusion in order to create a just climate future. Indeed, fit-for-purpose climate policy must be underpinned by a deep understanding of the barriers, capabilities, and opportunities of those who are likely to be adversely affected by the transition to Net Zero.

Changes to policymaking and implementation will be necessary to ensure a just transition to Net Zero – a new approach to policymaking must move away from siloed policy design and siloed funding. Further, across this book we have emphasized the significance of place, and the need for a place-based approach (see Middlemiss et al, 2024b for a focused discussion of this). We argue that this requires a partnership approach between local and national governments. In the UK context, while national government leadership risks creating 'place-blind' climate policy, investment and finance, local government is currently not sufficiently resourced, lacks capacity and lacks devolved powers. As such, policy for just climate futures requires a more integrated and distributed system of delivery and accountability. This is supported by literature on policymaking for so-called long emergencies (see Kunstler, 2006; Martin et al, 2023), as well as the participants in our research, who saw a range of stakeholders (including local and national policymakers) needing to take leadership for driving climate policy (The Young Foundation, 2024).

In this final section, we highlight the main policy changes needed to create and deliver the inclusive climate policy we proposed earlier. In sum, we argue that a *person-centred, place-based approach* to policy is needed (Middlemiss et al, 2024b), and that this requires coordination and action across and between local, regional and national government alongside key non-governmental actors. Given that the UK currently has a rather centralized policymaking system, we argue that successful policymaking and implementation requires a departure towards not just *devolution* of climate policy as we might currently understand it, but *distributed accountability*. Here we argue for distributed leadership for different key policy priorities. Our policy recommendations are as follows:

National government and policy

At the national policy level, policymakers should remove the most significant barriers for the poorest households and take a person-centred approach to design incentives that support participation in the transition. This includes providing economic support to cover the upfront costs of retrofit or changing transport, and to cushion changes to day-to-day costs of food, fuel and pricing. Such costs are unavoidable if the poorest households are to reach Net Zero, and policies for economic support must account for households' spending power and budget constraints. National government must also set clear policy and public direction on the public's role in Net Zero.

Devolved powers

Devolution is critical to delivering inclusive climate policy, and national and local government need to develop strong devolved governance for Net Zero policy with distributed powers. The precise solution is likely to vary – it may mean working at the regional policy level to address challenges that cut across local administrative areas, or working at the community, or even street level. Fundamentally, local areas must be recognized as having distinctive transition risks and opportunities. Further, local authority districts do not sit as isolated place entities – they are affected by the prosperity or decline, interconnected infrastructures, or climate impacts of their neighbouring districts, and by the nearest city that acts as a central hub for community and industrial opportunities.

Further exploration is needed to understand the precise organizational arrangements necessary to deliver the economic and infrastructural changes for a just transition to Net Zero. In the UK for example, this raises questions around whether the current system is best organized by local authority or by regional governance, to ensure there is sufficient capacity for leadership and action. The bottom line is that an integrated approach is needed for a just transition that focuses on understanding what works in different places. From there, it will be possible to develop tailored visions and plans for different geographic areas. This is likely to involve giving local authorities more power and establishing clear strategies for collaboration among local governments, key institutions, and community members.

Supporting community involvement and championship

Third, our research strongly indicates that motivation to get involved in Net Zero is stronger when connected to 'place' (see for example Middlemiss et al, 2024b), and when people are engaged in the design of local policy and development of future visions. Community involvement is essential to enable a place-focused, inclusive debate, to test place-based transition strategies to ensure they work for all, and to ensure a local democratic mandate for just climate futures. Community action must recognize the inequalities and injustices faced by specific groups and places and engage the public meaningfully in decision-making through local civic participation structures.

Data, monitoring and assessment

Fourth, existing bodies have an important role to play in how progress towards an inclusive low-carbon future is monitored, organized and assessed. For example, in the UK there is a need to update the existing Climate Change Committee (CCC) Risk Assessment to provide a picture of community and household vulnerabilities over the course of the Net Zero transition. This would mean extending the existing Assessment to fully account for different people and places, expanding its scope beyond hard infrastructure, and accounting for a much broader set of social, asset-based, social infrastructure measures. Such an assessment should drive a national strategy for public participation in a just transition. Local leaders, civic actors and investors also need support from the national government to build up local data infrastructure to aid monitoring. This investment will help adopt a data-driven approach that is place-appropriate. The Young Foundation's 'Index of Readiness for Net Zero' is a good example of a tool that helps pinpoint where local communities can accelerate progress on areas of high potential towards a just transition to Net Zero. It also highlights opportunities for action, and areas of risk and weakness.

Conclusion: Jim's just transition

Our previous chapter ended with Jim's story, identifying how he might struggle during the transition to Net Zero. We can now revisit this in Box 5.3, concluding with what a just climate future might look like in Jim's case given the recommendations we have made previously. In our discussion about how an inclusive just transition for Jim can be achieved, we use quotations from the people we met in Leeds and Newcastle to bring to life what more inclusive climate policy will mean for Jim and others like him.

Box 5.3: Jim's just climate future

What is life like now and how is Jim at risk?

We met Jim in Chapter 4, where we described his life as a car mechanic, living in a housing association flat, and in an area characterized by poor public transport links, limited job opportunities and social infrastructure. Given his job, he is likely to be strongly affected by the transition to electric vehicles, but this shift could also impact on his social life and his ability to look after his mum.

How can inclusive climate policy ensure a just transition?

Economic

One of our participants in Leeds talked about the challenges of not meeting government criteria for help. As he put it:

> We don't qualify for any of that. And that's a kick in the teeth for me. Because it's not like I've got the money for a lot of this stuff ... We spent a lot in the past 6 months to make a lot of improvements for the household ... now, I can't financially afford anything else.
>
> Quotation 27, Neighbourhood B, Leeds

Including Jim

Under new criteria shaped by just climate principles, Jim is supported financially to keep up with changes in green technology through a partnership scheme between government and EV market providers; and enhanced housing regulations ensure that Jim's landlord is willing and able to retrofit his home to a high standard. Jim's cost of living remains the same, or, potentially reduces given that he will benefit from tax breaks, and lower running costs of his EV.

Employment and skills

Many of our participants in Leeds and Newcastle were concerned about the feasibility of new employment in the transition, given how invisible retraining was in their everyday lives. As one explained:

> When I think one of the problems will be training people in the new industries ... certainly the building colleges are not yet really geared up to training people how to do a heat source pump, for automotive, how do you repair an electric vehicle? ... I've seen nothing about new jobs ... and new training ... everything's still clinging on to the olden days.
>
> Quotation 813, Neighbourhood A, Leeds

Including Jim

While Jim's job remains at risk during the transition to Net Zero, new policy on skills development means that he is offered local, affordable and accessible retraining through continuous professional development, delivered via the local further education college, that will qualify him to work on electric vehicles. Given the ever-increasing demand for these skills Jim is likely to have more opportunities for employment, with the potential for higher pay.

Social

There are big opportunities to build on existing community strengths to ensure that social participation is sustained. While we have been through some highly challenging years, people have learned resilience, which can be built on. As one participant put it:

> I think one of the good things about COVID is the community that I'm a part of now on our street is much tighter and much more supportive. A lot of recycling between the streets; you know, if someone's getting rid of something now we'll put it on the WhatsApp group.
>
> Quotation 302, Neighbourhood C, Leeds

Including Jim

For Jim, investment in the local community may also provide more local opportunities for leisure and social activities locally, further strengthening this resilience. A new leisure centre that he can walk to has also resulted in independent businesses setting up in his community, offering affordable fresh food options. Being more present in the community will give him more opportunities to learn informally about Net Zero policies – for example – energy efficiency 'life hacks'.

Political

Our participants were worried about the level of government commitment to change, and there is a strong need to grow trust in this process. One of our participants from Newcastle captured this:

> So, the bottom line for me is trust. Do I really trust these people [Newcastle Government] to do what they are promising? Am I just being roped into another scheme? Do you know what I mean? But it will be lovely, it will be beautiful.

There really are great plans for 2030 for all this. But again, I'm not sure if I trust them, you know.

> Quotation 510, Neighbourhood C, Newcastle

Including Jim

Since there has been clearer leadership from national government on Net Zero, local government publicly articulating their commitment, and measuring process, and greater community cohesion and opportunities to engage in local democracy, Jim has a voice in decision making, with greater ownership over policies, feeling like they are being made 'with' him rather than done 'to' him.

A just climate future

Jim's skills will be enhanced by accessible, affordable retraining to allow him to work in the EV industry. Financial support will mean that he can afford an EV himself (if he needs one) with the running costs of this much cheaper than a petrol car. Net Zero policies will not reduce his disposable income. Net Zero policies will enable the things he needs and values in his daily life: access to friends, family, leisure, shopping, and employment and training opportunities. Improved community cohesion, services, and facilities, as well as a diversified, more resilient economy, will make it easier to have a voice in local matters such as community-based energy decisions.

Notes

Chapter 2
1. This changed to the Department for Energy Security and Net Zero (DESNZ) in 2023.
2. Value Added Tax – a UK tax placed on goods/services purchased.
3. In the UK this has become a controversial issue, with the deadline extended to 2035 by then Prime Minister Rishi Sunak.
4. While substantial changes are anticipated within agricultural policy and land use policy, and we recognize the impact that this may have on food prices and other aspects of life such as employment, here we focus on aspects of food systems that have an immediate, direct impact on households.
5. While such spaces can provide amenity and leisure facilities, it can also protect populations from climatic events such as heatwaves (Climate Change Committee 2020a, 2020b).

Chapter 3
1. Note that we do not use this for the 'work life' section as there is no direct carbon footprint associated with this.
2. Often used interchangeably with the term 'energy poverty'. In essence it refers to a situation where a household cannot afford to use sufficient energy to meet its needs, or where it does, other aspects of life, such as buying food, are compromised.
3. See (Curtis and Lehner, 2019) for a discussion of definitions of this. In its broadest sense it refers to the sharing of skills, goods or services, either for money (for example, Airbnb or Uber) or for free (for example, Olio or freecycle).

Chapter 4
1. Rob White's work on Environmental Harm (2013) provides a valuable critique of the failures of environmental policy.

References

Aabø, S., Audunson, R. and Vårheim, A. (2010) How do public libraries function as meeting places? *Library & Information Science Research*, 32: 16–26.

Active Travel England (2024) £101 million investment to boost cycling and walking nationwide, Gov.uk [online], Available from: https://www.gov.uk/government/news/101-million-investment-to-boost-cycling-and-walking-nationwide#:~:text=The%20%C2%A3101%20million%20funding,2023%2F24%20and%202024%2F25

Adams, S., Kuch, D., Diamond, L., Fröhlich, P., Henriksen, I.M., Katzeff, C., Ryghaug, M. and Yilmaz, S. (2021) Social license to automate: a critical review of emerging approaches to electricity demand management, *Energy Research & Social Science*, 80: 102210.

Aldred, R. and Goodman, A. (2021) The impact of low traffic neighbourhoods on active travel, car use, and perceptions of local environment during the COVID-19 pandemic, *Transport Findings*, March, DOI: 10.32866/001c.21390

Ambrose, A., Baker, W., Sherriff, G. and Chambers, J. (2021) Cold comfort: Covid-19, lockdown and the coping strategies of fuel poor households, *Energy Reports*, 7: 5589–96.

Ambrosio-Albala, P., Middlemiss, L., Owen, A., Hargreaves, T., Emmel, N., Gilbertson, J., Tod, A., Snell, C., Mullen, C., Longhurst, N. and Gillard, R. (2020) From rational to relational: how energy poor households engage with the British retail energy market, *Energy Research & Social Science*, 70: 101765.

Anantharaman, M., Huddart Kennedy, E., Middlemiss, L. and Bradbury, S. (2019) Who participates in community-based sustainable consumption projects and why does it matter? A constructively critical approach, in: C. Isenhour, M. Martiskainen and L. Middlemiss (eds) *Power and Politics in Sustainable Consumption Research and Practice*, Abingdon: Routledge, pp 178–200.

Anderson, A.R. and Knee, E. (2021) Queer isolation or queering isolation? Reflecting upon the Ramifications of COVID-19 on the future of queer leisure spaces, *Leisure Sciences*, 43(1–2, Special Issue): 118–24.

APPG for Left Behind Neighbourhoods (2021) *Levelling Up through Climate Action: A Once in a Lifetime Opportunity to Make Sure No Neighbourhood is 'Left Behind'* [online], Available from: https://www.appg-leftbehindneighbourhoods.org.uk/publication/levelling-up-through-climate-action-a-once-in-a-lifetime-opportunity-to-make-sure-no-neighbourhood-is-left-behind/

Armstrong, C.M., Niinimäki, K., Kujala, S., Karell, E. and Lang, C. (2015) Sustainable product-service systems for clothing: exploring consumer perceptions of consumption alternatives in Finland. *Journal of Cleaner Production*, 97(Special volume): 30–9.

Arnold, T., Wong, C., Baker, M., Koksal, C., Baing, A.S. and Zheng, W. (2019) *Measuring Spatial Inequality in the UK: What We Know and What We Should Know?*, University of Manchester [online], Available from: https://research.manchester.ac.uk/en/publications/measuring-spatial-inequality-in-the-uk-what-we-know-and-what-we-s

Atkinson, A.B. (1998) Social exclusion, poverty and unemployment, in: A.B. Atkinson and J. Hills (eds) *Exclusion, Employment and Opportunity*, London: Centre for Analysis of Social Exclusion.

Bakhshi, H. and Schneider, P. (2017) *The Future of Skills: Employment in 2030*, London: Pearson.

Ballesteros-Arjona, V., Oliveras, L., Bolívar Muñoz, J., Olry de Labry Lima, A., Carrere, J., Martín Ruiz, E., et al (2022) What are the effects of energy poverty and interventions to ameliorate it on people's health and well-being? A scoping review with an equity lens, *Energy Research & Social Science*, 87: 102456.

Baltruszewicz, M., Steinberger, J.K., Paavola, J., Ivanova, D., Brand-Correa, L.I. and Owen, A. (2023) Social outcomes of energy use in the United Kingdom: household energy footprints and their links to well-being, *Ecological Economics*, 205, 107686.

Barbosa, O., Tratalos, J.A., Armsworth, P.R., Davies, R.G., Fuller, R.A., Johnson, P. and Gaston, K.J. (2007) Who benefits from access to green space? A case study from Sheffield, *Landscape and Urban Planning*, 83, 187–95.

Barrett, J., Pye, S., Betts-Davies, S., Eyre, N., Broad, O., Price, J., Norman, J., Anable, J., Bennett, G. and Brand, C. (2021) *The Role of Energy Demand Reduction in Achieving Net-Zero in the UK*, Oxford: Centre for Research into Energy Demand Solutions.

Bartiaux, F., Day, R. and Lahaye, W. (2021) Energy poverty as a restriction of multiple capabilities: a systemic approach for Belgium, *Journal of Human Development and Capabilities*, 22(2): 270–91.

BEIS (2021a) *Net Zero Strategy: Build Back Greener*, Gov.uk [online], Available from: https://www.webarchive.org.uk/access/resolve/20211031101659/https://assets.publishing.service.gov.uk/government/uploads/system/uploads/attachment_data/file/1028157/net-zero-strategy.pdf

BEIS (2021b) *Industrial Decarbonisation Strategy*, Gov.uk [online], Available from: https://assets.publishing.service.gov.uk/government/uploads/system/uploads/attachment_data/file/970229/Industrial_Decarbonisation_Strategy_March_2021.pdf

BEIS (2021c) Net Zero Public Engagement and Participation: A Research Note, Gov.uk [online], Available from: https://assets.publishing.service.gov.uk/government/uploads/system/uploads/attachment_data/file/969428/net-zero-public-engagement-participation-research-note.pdf

Belk, R. (2014) You are what you can access: sharing and collaborative consumption online, *Journal of Business Research*, 67: 1595–600.

Bernardi, M. and Diamantini, D. (2018) Shaping the sharing city: an exploratory study on Seoul and Milan, *Journal of Cleaner Production*, 203: 30–42.

Berry, A. (2019) The distributional effects of a carbon tax and its impact on fuel poverty: a microsimulation study in the French context, *Energy Policy*, 124: 81–94.

Birchley, G., Huxtable, R., Murtagh, M., ter Meulen, R., Flach, P. and Gooberman-Hill, R. (2017) Smart homes, private homes? An empirical study of technology researchers' perceptions of ethical issues in developing smart-home health technologies, *BMC Medical Ethics*, 18: 23.

Bohnenberger, K. (2020) Money, vouchers, public infrastructures? A framework for sustainable welfare benefits, *Sustainability*, 12: 596.

Bondemark, A., Andersson, H., Wretstrand, A. and Brundell-Freij, K. (2021) Is it expensive to be poor? Public transport in Sweden, *Transportation*, 48: 2709–34.

Boomsma, C., Hafner, R., Pahl, S., Jones, R.V. and Fuertes, A. (2018) Should we play games where energy is concerned? Perceptions of serious gaming as a technology to motivate energy behaviour change among social housing residents, *Sustainability*, 10(6): 1729.

Bosch, G. (2023) Employment policy for a just transition – the example of Germany, *Transfer: European Review of Labour & Research*, 29: 405–21.

Bouzarovski, S. and Simcock, N. (2017) Spatializing energy justice, *Energy Policy*, 107: 640–8.

Bowen, A. and Kuralbayeva, K. (2015) Looking for green jobs: the impact of green growth on employment, London: Grantham Research Institute on Climate Change and the Environment and Global Green Growth Institute Working Papers.

Brand-Correa, L.I. and Steinberger, J.K. (2017) A framework for decoupling human need satisfaction from energy use, *Ecological Economics*, 141: 43–52.

Bray, R. and Ford, R. (2021) Energy justice POINTs: policies to create a more sustainable & fairer future for all, University of Strathclyde [online], Available from: https://strathprints.strath.ac.uk/76421/

British Dietetic Association (2021) Policy statement: environmentally sustainable diets [online], Available from: https://www.bda.uk.com/static/9e8a51df-4954-496a-aadec4d0b73d77f9/c899cfa5-9b19-41a3-b221d34af6ec1f7e/policystatementsustainablefood.pdf

Broadband Commission (2022) Reducing inequality and achieving universal connectivity [online], Available from: https://www.broadbandcommission.org/insight/reducing-inequality-and-achieving-universal-connectivity/

Brundtland, G.H. (2005) *Our Common Future: Report of the World Commission on Environment and Development* (4th edn), Geneva: UN.

Büchs, M. (2021) Sustainable welfare: independence between growth and welfare has to go both ways, *Global Social Policy*, 21: 323–7.

Büchs, M. and Koch, M. (2017) *Postgrowth and Wellbeing*, Cham: Springer International.

Büchs, M. and Mattioli, G. (2021) Trends in air travel inequality in the UK: From the few to the many? *Travel Behaviour & Society*, 25, 92–101.

Buekers, J., Van Holderbeke, M., Bierkens, J. and Int Panis, L. (2014) Health and environmental benefits related to electric vehicle introduction in EU countries, *Transport Research Part D: Transport and Environment*, 33: 26–38.

Cain, L. and Moore, G. (2019) *Evaluation of Camden Council's Citizens' Assembly on the Climate Crisis*, London: UCL Culture, Engagement.

California Jobs Plan (2021) California's climate goals will create one million new jobs [online], Available from: https://www.californiaclimatejobsplan.com/jobscreation#:~:text=Investing%20%2476%20billion%20per%20year,per%20year%20in%20the%20state

Calver, P. and Simcock, N. (2021) Demand response and energy justice: a critical overview of ethical risks and opportunities within digital, decentralised, and decarbonised futures, *Energy Policy*, 151: 112198.

Calver, P., Mander, S. and Abi Ghanem, D. (2022) Low carbon system innovation through an energy justice lens: exploring domestic heat pump adoption with direct load control in the United Kingdom, *Energy Research & Social Science*, 83: 102299.

Caplan, P. (2017) Win-win? Food poverty, food aid and food surplus in the UK today, *Anthropology Today*, 33(3): 17–22.

CBC News (2023) Canada lays out plan to phase out sales of gas-powered cars, trucks by 2035 [online], Available from: https://www.cbc.ca/news/politics/canada-electric-vehicles-2035-1.7063993

Centre for Research in Social Policy (2021) Minimum income standard [online], Available from: https://www.lboro.ac.uk/research/crsp/minimum-income-standard/

Centre for Research into Energy Demand Solutions, Pye, S., Betts-Davies, S., Eyre, N., Broad, O., Price, J., Norman, J., et al (2021) The role of energy demand reduction in achieving net-zero in the UK [online], Available from: https://www.creds.ac.uk/wp-content/uploads/CREDS-Role-of-energy-demand-report-2021.pdf

Chapman, A. and Okushima, S. (2019) Engendering an inclusive low-carbon energy transition in Japan: considering the perspectives and awareness of the energy poor, *Energy Policy*, 135: 111017.

Chzhen, Y. (2017) Unemployment, social protection spending and child poverty in the European Union during the Great Recession, *Journal of European Social Policy*, 27: 123–37.

City Plants (2020) Plant free trees in your neighborhood [online], Available from: https://plan.mayor.lacity.gov/sites/g/files/wph2176/files/2022-12/Plant_Free_Trees_in_Your_Neighborhood.pdf

Clapp, J. and Ruder, S.-L. (2020) Precision technologies for agriculture: digital farming, gene-edited crops, and the politics of sustainability, *Global Environmental Politics*, 20: 49–69.

Clapp, J. and Scrinis, G. (2017) Big food, nutritionism, and corporate power, *Globalizations*, 14: 578–95.

Clapp, J., Noyes, I. and Grant, Z. (2021) The food systems summit's failure to address corporate power, *Development*, 64: 192–8.

Climate Assembly UK (2020) *The Path to Net Zero: Climate Assembly UK Full Report* [online], Available from: https://www.climateassembly.uk/report/read/final-report.pdf

Climate Change Committee (2020a) *The Sixth Carbon Budget: The UK's Path to Net Zero* [online], Available from: https://www.theccc.org.uk/publication/sixth-carbon-budget/

Climate Change Committee (2020b) *Policies for the Sixth Carbon Budget and Net Zero* [online], Available from: https://www.theccc.org.uk/wp-content/uploads/2020/12/Policies-for-the-Sixth-Carbon-Budget-and-Net-Zero.pdf

Climate Change Committee (2021) *Joint Recommendations: 2021 Report to Parliament* [online], Available from: https://www.theccc.org.uk/wp-content/uploads/2021/06/CCC-Joint-Recommendations-2021-Report-to-Parliament.pdf

Climate Change Committee (2023) *A Net Zero Workforce* [online], Available from: https://www.theccc.org.uk/wp-content/uploads/2023/05/CCC-A-Net-Zero-Workforce-Web.pdf

Colding, J., Barthel, S., Ljung, R., Eriksson, F. and Sjöberg, S. (2022) Urban commons and collective action to address climate change, *Social Inclusion*, 10: 103–14.

Consumer Data Research Centre (2024) Index of Multiple Deprivation [online], Available from: https://data.cdrc.ac.uk/dataset/index-multiple-deprivation-imd

Conway, L. (2021) *Right to Repair Regulations: Research Briefing* [online], Available from: https://commonslibrary.parliament.uk/research-briefings/cbp-9302/

Cook, J., Nuccitelli, D., Green, S.A., Richardson, M., Winkler, B., Painting, R., Way, R., Jacobs, P. and Skuce, A. (2013) Quantifying the consensus on anthropogenic global warming in the scientific literature, Environmental Research Letters, 8: 024024.

Corfe, S. and Keohane, N. (2018) *Measuring the Poverty Premium*, London: Social Market Foundation.

Crenshaw, K. (1991) Mapping the margins: intersectionality, identity politics, and violence against women of color, *Stanford Law Review*, 43: 1241.

Cribb, J., Waters, T., Wernham, T. and Xu, X. (2021) *Living Standards, Poverty and Inequality in the UK: 2021*, London: Institute for Fiscal Studies.

Curtis, S.K. and Lehner, M. (2019) Defining the sharing economy for sustainability, *Sustainability*, 11: 567.

Davenport, A. and Zaranko, B. (2020) Levelling Up: Where and How? [online], Available from: https://ifs.org.uk/publications/15055.

Davies, S. and Trend, L. (2020) *The Poverty Premium: A Customer Perspective*, Bristol: University of Bristol.

Davies, S., Finney, A. and Hartfree, Y. (2016) *Paying to be Poor: Uncovering the Scale and Nature of the Poverty Premium*, Bristol: University of Bristol.

Davis, A., Hirsch, D., Padley, M. and Shepherd, C. (2021) *A Minimum Income Standard for the United Kingdom in 2021*, York: Joseph Rowntree Foundation.

Davis, O. and Geiger, B.B. (2017) Did food insecurity rise across Europe after the 2008 crisis? An analysis across welfare regimes, *Social Policy & Society*, 16: 343–60.

Davis, S.J., Lewis, N.S., Shaner, M., Aggarwal, S., Arent, D., Azevedo, I.L., et al (2018) Net-zero emissions energy systems, *Science*, 360: eaas9793.

DEFRA (2020) *Straws, Cotton Buds and Drink Stirrers Ban: Rules for Businesses in England*, Gov.uk [online], Available from: https://www.gov.uk/guidance/straws-cotton-buds-and-drink-stirrers-ban-rules-for-businesses-in-england.

DEFRA (2022) *A Review of Public Engagement, Covering Concepts, Practices and Experience of Public Engagement*, Gov.uk [online], Available from: https://www.gov.uk/government/publications/review-of-public-engagement

DESNZ (2023) Domestic private rented property: minimum energy efficiency standard - landlord guidance, Gov.uk [online], Available from: https://www.gov.uk/guidance/domestic-private-rented-property-minimum-energy-efficiency-standard-landlord-guidance

Devaney, L., Brereton, P., Torney, D., Coleman, M., Boussalis, C. and Coan, T.G. (2020) Environmental literacy and deliberative democracy: a content analysis of written submissions to the Irish Citizens' Assembly on climate change, *Climate Change*, 162: 1965–84.

DfT (2021a) *Decarbonising Transport: A Better, Greener Britain* [online], Available from: https://assets.publishing.service.gov.uk/media/610d63ffe90e0706d92fa282/decarbonising-transport-a-better-greener-britain.pdf

DfT (2021b) *Vehicle Licensing Statistics: April to June 2021* [online], Available from: https://www.gov.uk/government/collections/vehicles-statistics

Dimbleby, H. (2021) *National Food Strategy Independent Review: The Plan*, London: HMSO.

DLUHC (2022) *Levelling Up the United Kingdom*, London: Department of Levelling Up, Housing and Communities.

Doherty, B., Saunders, C. and Hayes, G. (2020) A new climate movement? Extinction rebellion's activists in profile, *CUSP Working Paper Series*, 25: 1–39.

Doran, A., El-Geneidy, A. and Manaugh, K. (2021) The pursuit of cycling equity: a review of Canadian transport plans, *Journal of Transport Geography*, 90: 102927.

Dowler, E. and Lambie-Mumford, H. (2015) How can households eat in austerity? Challenges for social policy in the UK, *Social Policy & Society*, 14: 417–28.

Druckman, A. and Jackson, T. (2009) The carbon footprint of UK households 1990–2004: a socio-economically disaggregated, quasi-multi-regional input–output model, *Ecological Economics*, 68: 2066–77.

DWP (2023) Households below average income: an analysis of the UK income distribution: FYE 1995 to FYE 2022 [online], Available from: https://www.gov.uk/government/statistics/households-below-average-income-for-financial-years-ending-1995-to-2022/households-below-average-income-an-analysis-of-the-uk-income-distribution-fye-1995-to-fye-2022

EAT-Lancet Commission (2021) *Healthy Diets from Sustainable Food Systems: Food Planet Health* [online], Available from: https://eatforum.org/content/uploads/2019/07/EAT-Lancet_Commission_Summary_Report.pdf

El Hachem, W. and De Giovanni, P. (2019) Accelerating the transition to alternative fuel vehicles through a Distributive Justice perspective, *Transport Research Part D: Transport and Environment*, 75: 72–86.

Elena-Bucea, A., Cruz-Jesus, F., Oliveira, T. and Coelho, P.S. (2021) Assessing the role of age, education, gender and income on the digital divide: evidence for the European Union, *Information Systems Frontiers*, 23: 1007–21.

Energy Saving Trust (2025) Cavity wall insulation [online], Available from: https://energysavingtrust.org.uk/advice/cavity-wall-insulation/

Environment Agency (2022) Environment Agency and climate change adaptation, Gov.uk [online], Available from: https://www.gov.uk/government/collections/environment-agency-and-climate-change-adaptation

European Commission (2024) Reducing emissions from aviation [online], Available from: https://climate.ec.europa.eu/eu-action/transport/reducing-emissions-aviation_en

European Parliament (2022) EU Ban on the sale of new petrol and diesel cars from 2035 explained [online], Available from: https://www.europarl.europa.eu/topics/en/article/20221019STO44572/eu-ban-on-sale-of-new-petrol-and-diesel-cars-from-2035-explained

Evans, G. and Phelan, L. (2016) Transition to a post-carbon society: linking environmental justice and just transition discourses, *Energy Policy*, 99: 329–39.

Fairness Foundation (2024) New polling shows concern about inequality extends beyond regional inequalities [online], Available from: https://files.fairnessfoundation.com/unequal-kingdom.pdf

Family Action (2013) Home economics: how families struggle to move into and maintain their homes [online], Available from: https://www.family-action.org.uk/content/uploads/2014/06/Family-Fortunes_Home-Economics.pdf

Fankhauser, S., Bowen, A., Calel, R., Dechezleprêtre, A., Grover, D., Rydge, J. and Sato, M. (2013) Who will win the green race? In search of environmental competitiveness and innovation, *Global Environmental Change*, 23: 902–13.

FAO (2024) *Hunger and Food Insecurity* [online], Available from: https://www.fao.org/hunger/en/#:~:text=A%20person%20is%20food%20insecure,at%20different%20levels%20of%20severity

Fecht, D., Fischer, P., Fortunato, L., Hoek, G., de Hoogh, K., Marra, M., et al (2015) Associations between air pollution and socioeconomic characteristics, ethnicity and age profile of neighbourhoods in England and the Netherlands, *Environmental Pollution*, 198: 201–10.

Fell, M.J. (2021) Anticipating distributional impacts of peer-to-peer energy trading: inference from a realist review of evidence on Airbnb, *Cleaner and Responsible Consumption*, 2: 100013.

Fenney, D. and Snell, C. (2011) Exceptions to the green rule? A literature investigation into the overlaps between the academic and UK policy fields of disability and the environment. *Local Environment*, 16(3): 251–64.

Fenney Salkeld, D. (2016) Sustainable lifestyles for all? Disability equality, sustainability and the limitations of current UK policy, *Disability & Society*, 31, 447–64.

Fielding, K.S. and Hornsey, M.J. (2016) A social identity analysis of climate change and environmental attitudes and behaviors: insights and opportunities, *Frontiers in Psychology*, 7: 1–12.

Fitzpatrick, S., Bramley, G., Sosenko, F., Blenkinsopp, J., Wood, J., Johnsen, S., et al (2018) *Destitution in the UK 2018*. York: Joseph Rowntree Found.

Food Packaging Forum (2021) *Chile Passes Comprehensive Plastics Legislation* [online], Available from: https://foodpackagingforum.org/news/chile-passes-comprehensive-plastics-legislation

Friends of the Earth (2020) *England's Green Space Gap* [online], Available from: https://friendsoftheearth.uk/nature/access-green-space-england-are-you-missing-out

Froy, F. and Giguère, S. (2010) *Breaking out of Policy Silos: Doing More with Less*, Paris: OECD.

Fuso Nerini, F., Fawcett, T., Parag, Y. and Ekins, P. (2021) Personal carbon allowances revisited, *Nature Sustainability*, 4: 1025–31.

Gadema, Z. and Oglethorpe, D. (2011) The use and usefulness of carbon labelling food: a policy perspective from a survey of UK supermarket shoppers, *Food Policy*, 36: 815–22.

Gallizzi, B. (2023) Arguments over energy usage on the rise in UK households [online], Available from: https://www.uswitch.com/gas-electricity/news/arguments-over-energy-usage-on-the-rise-in-uk-households/

Garvey, A. and Taylor, P. (2020) *Industrial Decarbonisation Policies for a UK Net Zero Target*. Centre for Research into Energy Demands Solutions [online], Available from: https://www.theccc.org.uk/wp-content/uploads/2020/12/CREDS-Industrial-decarbonisation-policies-for-a-UK-Net-Zero-target.pdf

Garvey, A., Norman, J., Owen, A. and Barrett, J. (2021) Towards net zero nutrition: the contribution of demand-side change to mitigating UK food emissions, *Journal of Cleaner Production*, 290: 125672.

Gasana, J., Dillikar, D., Mendy, A., Forno, E. and Ramos Vieira, E. (2012) Motor vehicle air pollution and asthma in children: a meta-analysis, *Environmental Research*, 117: 36–45.

Gasparrini, A., Guo, Y., Sera, F., Vicedo-Cabrera, A.M., Huber, V., Tong, S., et al (2017) Projections of temperature-related excess mortality under climate change scenarios, *Lancet Planetary Health*, 1: e360–7.

Geissinger, A., Laurell, C., Öberg, C. and Sandström, C. (2019) How sustainable is the sharing economy? On the sustainability connotations of sharing economy platforms, *Journal of Cleaner Production*, 206: 419–29.

Gillard, R., Snell, C. and Bevan, M. (2017) Advancing an energy justice perspective of fuel poverty: household vulnerability and domestic retrofit policy in the United Kingdom, *Energy Research & Social Science*, 29: 53–61.

Gius, C. (2021) Online communities as points of observation of the transnational migrant career: a case study on Italian immigrants in Toronto, *Journal of Ethnic and Migration Studies*, 47: 2634–49.

Gornig, M. and Goebel, J. (2018) Deindustrialisation and the polarisation of household incomes: the example of urban agglomerations in Germany, *Urban Studies*, 55: 790–806.

Gössling, S. (2016) Urban transport justice, *Journal of Transport Geography*, 54: 1–9.

Gough, I. (2011) *New Paradigms In Public Policy: Climate Change and Public Policy Futures*, London: British Academy Policy Centre.

Gough, I. (2015) Climate change and sustainable welfare: the centrality of human needs, *Cambridge Journal of Economics*, 39: 1191–214.

Gough, I. (2022) Two scenarios for sustainable welfare: a framework for an eco-social contract, *Social Policy & Society*, 21: 460–72.

Governor Newsom's Office (2022) California releases world's first plan to achieve Net Zero carbon pollution [online], Available from: https://www.gov.ca.gov/2022/11/16/california-releases-worlds-first-plan-to-achieve-net-zero-carbon-pollution/

Green Economy Tracker (2024a) Sweden: Inclusion driving green ambition [online], Available from: https://greeneconomytracker.org/country/sweden

Green Economy Tracker (2024b) New Zealand: Aotearoa's ambition on alternative economy [online], Available from: https://greeneconomytracker.org/country/new-zealand

Griffiths, M.L., Gray, B.J., Kyle, R.G. and Davies, A.R. (2022) Exploring the health impacts and inequalities of the new way of working: findings from a cross-sectional study (preprint), *Public and Global Health*, DOI: 10.1101/2022.01.07.22268797

Grossmann, M. and Creamer, E. (2016) Assessing diversity and inclusivity within the Transition movement: an urban case study, *Environmental Politics*, 26: 161–82.

Gundersen, C. and Gruber, J. (2001) The dynamic determinants of food insufficiency, in: M. Andrews and M. Prell (eds) *Second Food Security Measurement and Research Conference, Volume II: Papers*, USDA, ERS Food Assistance and Nutrition Research Report No. 11-2: 91–110.

Gundersen, C. and Ziliak, J.P. (2014) *Childhood Food Insecurity in the US: Trends, Causes, and Policy Options. The Future of Children Research Report*, Princeton, NJ: The Future of Children.

Guy, C., Clarke, G. and Eyre, H. (2004) Food retail change and the growth of food deserts: a case study of Cardiff, *International Journal of Retail & Distribution Management*, 32: 72–88.

Haas, T. (2021) The political economy of mobility justice, experiences from Germany, *Mobilities*, 17(6): 899–913.

Hajat, S., Vardoulakis, S., Heaviside, C. and Eggen, B. (2014) Climate change effects on human health: projections of temperature-related mortality for the UK during the 2020s, 2050s and 2080s, *Journal of Epidemiology and Community Health*, 68: 641–8.

Hargittai, E., Piper, A.M. and Morris, M.R. (2019) From internet access to internet skills: digital inequality among older adults, *Universal Access in the Information Society*, 18: 881–90.

Hargreaves, T. and Middlemiss, L. (2020) The importance of social relations in shaping energy demand, *Nature Energy*, 5: 195–201.

Hasegawa, T., Fujimori, S., Havlík, P., Valin, H., Bodirsky, B.L., Doelman, J.C., et al (2018) Risk of increased food insecurity under stringent global climate change mitigation policy, *Nature Climate Change*, 8: 699–703.

Haushofer, J. and Fehr, E. (2014) On the psychology of poverty, *Science*, 344: 862–7.

Health Expert Advisory Group (2020) Sustainable health equity: achieving a Net-Zero UK [online], Available from: https://www.theccc.org.uk/wp-content/uploads/2020/11/Sustainable-Health-Equity-Achieving-a-Net-Zero-UK-report-FINAL.pdf

Healy, N. and Barry, J. (2017) Politicizing energy justice and energy system transitions: fossil fuel divestment and a 'just transition', *Energy Policy*, 108: 451–9.

Henderson, J. (2020) EVs are not the answer: a mobility justice critique of Electric Vehicle Transitions, *Annals of the American Association of Geographers*, 110: 1993–2010.

HM Treasury (2021) Net Zero Review: Analysis exploring the key issues, Gov.uk [online], Available from: https://assets.publishing.service.gov.uk/government/uploads/system/uploads/attachment_data/file/1026725/NZR_-_Final_Report_-_Published_version.pdf

HM Treasury (2023) New UK levy to level carbon pricing, Gov.uk [online], Available from: https://www.gov.uk/government/news/new-uk-levy-to-level-carbon-pricing

Hoffmann, E., Barros, H. and Ribeiro, A. (2017) Socioeconomic inequalities in green space quality and accessibility – evidence from a Southern European city, *International Journal of Environmental Research and Public Health*, 14: 916.

Hoole, C., Collinson, S. and Newman, J. (2023) England's Catch-22: institutional limitations to achieving balanced growth through devolution, *Contemporary Social Science*, 18: 428–48.

House of Commons Committee of Public Accounts (2024) Cross working: twelfth report of session 2023-2024 [online], Available from: https://committees.parliament.uk/publications/43286/documents/215470/default/

Hubacek, K., Baiocchi, G., Feng, K., Castillo, R.M., Sun, L. and Xue, J. (2017) Global carbon inequality, *Energy, Ecology and Environment*, 2: 361–9.

Hur, E. (2020) Rebirth fashion: secondhand clothing consumption values and perceived risks, *Journal of Cleaner Production*, 273: 122951.

Hussein, Z., Hertel, T. and Golub, A. (2013) Climate change mitigation policies and poverty in developing countries, *Environmental Research Letters*, 8, 035009.

Huwe, V. (2021) Whose streets? Justice in transport decarbonization and gender, Ifso Working Paper Series 13, University of Duisburg-Essen: Institute for Socioeconomics (ifso) [online], Available from: https://ideas.repec.org/p/zbw/ifsowp/13.html

IFS (2022) *Geographies of Socio-economic Inequality* [online], Available from: https://ifs.org.uk/inequality/wp-content/uploads/2022/02/Geographies-of-socio-economic-inequality-IFS-Deaton-Review-Inequalities.pdf

IFS (2024) *The Labour Market* [online], Available from: https://ifs.org.uk/inequality/themes/the-labour-market/

ILO (2015) Guidelines for a just transition towards environmentally sustainable economies and societies for all, International Labour Organization [online], Available from: https://www.ilo.org/wcmsp5/groups/public/@ed_emp/@emp_ent/documents/publication/wcms_432859.pdf

Institute for Community Studies (2020) *Safety in Numbers? A Research Agenda with Communities, for Communities* [online], Available from: https://icstudies.org.uk/sites/default/files/uploads/files/RESEARCH%20AGENDA%20V6g.pdf

Institute for Sustainable Infrastructure (2023) Los Angeles River Way, San Fernando Valley completion project (Vanalden to Balboa) [online], Available from: https://sustainableinfrastructure.org/project-awards/los-angeles-river-way-san-fernando-valley-completion-project-vanalden-to-balboa/

International Transport Forum (2020) Zero car growth: a challenge for transport justice (International Transport Forum Discussion Papers No. 2020/12), Paris: OECD.

IPCC (2018) Summary for policymakers of IPCC Special Report on Global Warming of 1.5°C approved by governments [online], Available from: https://www.ipcc.ch/2018/10/08/summary-for-policymakers-of-ipcc-special-report-on-global-warming-of-1-5c-approved-by-governments/

IPCC (2022) *Climate Change 2022: Impacts, Adaptation and Vulnerability*, Cambridge: Cambridge University Press.

IPPR (2017) Net-Zero North: delivering the decarbonisation mission in the north of England, Institute for Public Policy Research [online], Available from: https://www.ippr.org/articles/net-zero-north

IPPR (2018) *Risk or Reward: Securing a Just Transition in the North of England*, Institute for Public Policy Research [online], Available from: https://www.ippr.org/publications/risk-or-reward

IPPR (2019) *A Just Transition: Realising the Opportunities of Decarbonisation in the North of England Final Report*, Institute for Public Policy Research [online], Available from: https://www.ippr.org/articles/a-just-transition

IPPR (2023) *State of the North 2023* [online], Available from: https://ippr-org.files.svdcdn.com/production/Downloads/looking-out-to-level-up-state-of-the-north-2023.pdf

IPPR (2024) *Skills Matter: Shaping A Just Transition For Workers in The Energy Sector* [online], Available from: https://ippr-org.files.svdcdn.com/production/Downloads/Skills_matter_May24.pdf

Ivanova, D. and Wood, R. (2020) The unequal distribution of household carbon footprints in Europe and its link to sustainability, *Global Sustainability*, 3: e18.

Ivanova, D. and Middlemiss, L. (2021) Characterizing the energy use of disabled people in the European Union towards inclusion in the energy transition, *Nature Energy*, 6: 1188–97.

Jeffres, L.W., Bracken, C.C., Jian, G. and Casey, M.F. (2009) The impact of third places on community quality of life, *Applied Research in Quality of Life*, 4: 333–45.

Jennings, N., Fecht, D. and De Matteis, S. (2019) Co-benefits of climate change mitigation in the UK, Grantham Institute Briefing Paper, 31, London: Imperial College London.

Johnson, C. (2020) Is demand side response a woman's work? Domestic labour and electricity shifting in low income homes in the United Kingdom, *Energy Research & Social Science*, 68: 101558.

Just Food (2024) *The Road to Net Zero – Big Food's Emissions Pledges* [online], Available from: https://www.just-food.com/features/the-road-to-net-zero-big-foods-emission-pledges/?cf-view

Just Transition Centre (2017) *Just Transition: A Report for the OECD*, Paris: OECD.

Kapetaniou, C. and McIvor, C. (2020) *Going Green: Preparing the UK Workforce for the Transition to a Net-Zero Economy*, NESTA [online], Available from: https://media.nesta.org.uk/documents/Going_Green-_Preparing_the_UK_workforce_to_the_transition_to_a_net_zero_economy.June.2020.pdf

Kelly, J.A., Clinch, J.P., Kelleher, L. and Shahab, S. (2020) Enabling a just transition: a composite indicator for assessing home-heating energy-poverty risk and the impact of environmental policy measures, *Energy Policy*, 146: 111791.

Kennedy, K. and Snell, C. (2023) Relationships between supermarkets and food charities in reducing food insecurity: lessons learned, *Voluntary Sector Review*, 1–10.

Kim, B.F., Santo, R.E., Scatterday, A.P., Fry, J.P., Synk, C.M., Cebron, S.R., et al (2020) Country-specific dietary shifts to mitigate climate and water crises, *Global Environmental Change*, 62: 101926.

King, D. (2020) *Zero Car Growth: A Challenge for Transport Justice*, International Transport Forum Discussion Papers No. 2020/12, Paris: OECD.

Kings College London (2024) *Public Perceptions on Climate Change*, London: The Policy Institute.

Koch, M. and Fritz, M. (2014) Building the eco-social state: do welfare regimes matter?, *Journal of Social Policy*, 43: 679–703.

Koskela, H. and Pain, R. (2000) Revisiting fear and place: women's fear of attack and the built environment, *Geoforum*, 31: 269–80.

Kunstler, J.H. (2006) *The Long Emergency: Surviving the End of Oil, Climate Change, and Other Converging Catastrophes of the Twenty-First Century*, New York: Grove Press.

Larrington-Spencer, H., Fenney, D., Middlemiss, L. and Kosanic, A. (2021) Disabled environmentalisms, in: K. Bell (ed) *Inclusion and Diversity in Environmentalism*, Abingdon: Routledge.

Lee, K.-T., Tsai, J.-Y., Hoang, A.T., Chen, W.-H., Gunarathne, D.S., Tran, K.-Q., Selvarajoo, A. and Goodarzi, V. (2022) Energy-saving drying strategy of spent coffee grounds for co-firing fuel by adding biochar for carbon sequestration to approach Net Zero, *Fuel*, 326: 124984.

Levitas, R., Pantazis, C., Fahmy, E., Gordon, D., Lloyd-Reichling, E. and Patsios, D. (2007) The multi-dimensional analysis of social exclusion, University of East London [online], Available from: https://repository.uel.ac.uk/item/8666q

LGA (2022) Climate Change Hub [online], Available from: https://www.local.gov.uk/our-support/climate-change-hub

Lisauskaite, E., McIntosh, S., Speckesser, S. and Espinoza, H. (2021) *Going Further: Further Education, Disadvantage and Social Mobility*, London: Centre for Vocational Education Research and The Sutton Trust.

Lister, R. (2016) Citizenship, welfare rights, in: J. Demaine and H. Entwistle (eds) *Beyond Communitarianism: Citizenship, Politics and Education*, London: Macmillan, p 163.

Lister, R. (2021) *Poverty* (2nd edn), Cambridge: Polity Press.

Loopstra, R. and Lalor, D. (2017) *Financial Insecurity, Food Insecurity, and Disability: The Profile of People Receiving Emergency Food Assistance from The Trussell Trust Network in Britain*, Salisbury: The Trussell Trust.

Loopstra, R., Reeves, A. and Tarasuk, V. (2019) The rise of hunger among low-income households: an analysis of the risks of food insecurity between 2004 and 2016 in a population-based study of UK adults, *Journal of Epidemiology and Community Health*, 73: 668–73.

Loopstra, R., Reeves, A., McKee, M. and Stuckler, D. (2016) Food insecurity and social protection in Europe: quasi-natural experiment of Europe's great recessions 2004–2012, *Preventative Medicine*, 89, 44–50.

Loopstra, R., Fledderjohann, J., Reeves, A. and Stuckler, D. (2018) Impact of welfare benefit sanctioning on food insecurity: a dynamic cross-area study of food bank usage in the UK, *Journal of Social Policy*, 47: 437–57.

Lubitow, A., Abelson, M.J. and Carpenter, E. (2020) Transforming mobility justice: gendered harassment and violence on transit, *Journal of Transport Geography*, 82: 102601.

Lucas, K. (2012) Transport and social exclusion: Where are we now? *Transport Policy*, 20: 105–13.

Lucas, K. and Musso, A. (2014) Policies for social inclusion in transportation: an introduction to the special issue, *Case Studies on Transport Policy*, 2: 37–40.

Lucas, K. and Pangbourne, K. (2014) Assessing the equity of carbon mitigation policies for transport in Scotland, *Case Studies on Transport Policy*, 2: 70–80.

Lucas, K., Stokes, G., Bastiaanssen, J. and Burkinshaw, J. (2019) *Inequalities in Mobility and Access in the UK Transport System*, Government Office for Science [online], Available from: https://assets.publishing.service.gov.uk/media/5c828f80ed915d07c9e363f7/future_of_mobility_access.pdf

Malka, L., Bidaj, F., Kuriqi, A., Jaku, A., Roçi, R. and Gebremedhin, A. (2023) Energy system analysis with a focus on future energy demand projections: the case of Norway, *Energy*, 272: 127107.

Mandelli, M. (2022) Understanding eco-social policies: a proposed definition and typology, *Transfer: European Review of Labour and Research*, 28: 333–48.

Mangold, H. and von Vacano, B. (2022) The frontier of plastics recycling: rethinking waste as a resource for high-value applications, *Macromolecular Chemistry and Physics*, 223: 2100488.

Markkanen, S. and Anger-Kraavi, A. (2019) Social impacts of climate change mitigation policies and their implications for inequality, *Climate Policy*, 19: 827–44.

Martin, C., Kan, H. and Fink, M. (2023) *Crisis Preparation In The Age Of Long Emergencies: What Covid-19 Teaches Us About the Capacity, Capability and Coordination Governments Need for Cross-cutting Crises*, Blavatnik School of Government and University of Oxford [online], Available from: https://www.bsg.ox.ac.uk/sites/default/files/2023-03/BSG-Crisis-preparation-age-long-emergencies.pdf

Marmot, M. and Allen, J. (2020) COVID-19: exposing and amplifying inequalities, *Journal of Epidemiology and Community Health*, 74: 681.

Marmot, M., Allen, J., Goldblatt, P., Herd, E. and Morrison, J. (2020) *Build Back Fairer: The COVID-19 Marmot Review*, London: UCL Institute of Health Equity.

Marmot Review Team (2011) *The Health Impacts of Cold Homes and Fuel Poverty*, London: Friends of the Earth & the Marmot Review Team.

Martin, C.J. (2016) The sharing economy: a pathway to sustainability or a nightmarish form of neoliberal capitalism? *Ecological Economics*, 121: 149–59.

Martinez, M., Wacket, M. and Abnett, K. (2023) Germany forms alliance to change EU's planned combustion engine ban, Reuters [online], Available from: https://www.reuters.com/world/europe/germany-forms-alliance-against-phase-out-internal-combustion-engines-by-2035-2023-03-13/

Martinus, K. (2018) Inequality and regional development in resource economies of advanced capitalist economies, *Geography Compass*, 12: e12405.

Martiskainen, M., Sovacool, B.K. and Hook, A. (2021) Temporality, consumption, and conflict: exploring user-based injustices in European low-carbon transitions, *Technology Analysis & Strategic Management*, 33: 770–82.

Mattioli, G., Lucas, K. and Marsden, G. (2017) Transport poverty and fuel poverty in the UK: from analogy to comparison, *Transport Policy*, 59: 93–105.

Mattioli, G., Morton, C. and Scheiner, J. (2021) Air travel and urbanity: the role of migration, social networks, airport accessibility, and 'rebound', *Urban Planning*, 6(2), DOI: 10.17645/up.v6i2.3983

Mazur, C., Contestabile, M., Offer, G.J. and Brandon, N.P. (2015) Assessing and comparing German and UK transition policies for electric mobility, *Environmental Innovation and Societal Transitions*, 14: 84–100.

McBride, K. and Purcell, S. (2014) *Food, Fuel, Finance: Tackling the Poverty Premium*, Church Action on Poverty [online], Available from: https://www.church-poverty.org.uk/wp-content/uploads/2019/06/Food-Fuel-Finance-report.pdf

McCabe, S. (2009) Who needs a holiday? Evaluating social tourism, *Annals of Tourism Research*, 36: 667–88.

McCauley, D. and Heffron, R. (2018) Just transition: integrating climate, energy and environmental justice, *Energy Policy*, 119: 1–7.

McGinn, A. and Isenhour, C. (2021) Negotiating the future of the adaptation fund: on the politics of defining and defending justice in the post-Paris Agreement period, *Climate Policy*, 21: 383–95.

McInroy, L.B. and Craig, S.L. (2020) 'It's like a safe haven fantasy world': online fandom communities and the identity development activities of sexual and gender minority youth, *Psychology of Popular Media*, 9: 236–46.

McIntyre, L. (2003) Food security: more than a determinant of health, *Policy Options*, 23: 46–51.

Mears, M., Brindley, P., Maheswaran, R. and Jorgensen, A. (2019) Understanding the socioeconomic equity of publicly accessible greenspace distribution: the example of Sheffield, UK *Geoforum*, 103: 126–37.

Middlemiss, L. and Gillard, R. (2015) Fuel poverty from the bottom-up: characterising household energy vulnerability through the lived experience of the fuel poor, Energy Research & Social Science, 6: 146–54.

Middlemiss, L., Ambrosio-Albalá, P., Emmel, N., Gillard, R., Gilbertson, J., Hargreaves, T., et al (2019) Energy poverty and social relations: a capabilities approach, *Energy Research & Social Science*, 55: 227–35.

Middlemiss, L., Snell, C., Morrison, E., Chzhen, Y., Owen, A., Kennedy, K., Theminimule, S. and Carregha, T. (2023) Conceptualising socially inclusive environmental policy: a just transition to Net Zero, *Social Policy and Society*, 22(4): 763–83.

Middlemiss, L., Davis, M., Brown, D., Bookbinder, R., Cairns, I., Mininni, G.M., et al (2024a) Developing a relational approach to energy demand: a methodological and conceptual guide, *Energy Research & Social Science*, 110(1 April): 103441.

Middlemiss, L., Snell, C., Theminimule, S., Carregha, T., Morrison, E., Chzhen, Y., Owen, A. and Kennedy, K. (2024b) Place-based and people-centred: principles for a socially inclusive net zero transition, *Geography and Environment*, 11(2), DOI: 10.1002/geo2.157

Millward-Hopkins, J., Steinberger, J.K., Rao, N.D. and Oswald, Y. (2020) Providing decent living with minimum energy: a global scenario, *Global Environmental Change*, 65: 102168.

Minaker, L.M. (2016) Retail food environments in Canada: maximizing the impact of research, policy and practice, *Canadian Journal of Public Health*, 107: eS1–3.

Ministry of Environment/Korean Environment Institute (2016) *Eco Label Certification System in Korea* [online], Available from: https://www.greenpolicyplatform.org/sites/default/files/downloads/policy-database/Korea%20Environmental%20Policy%20Bulletin%20-%20Eco-label%20Certification%20System%20(ECS)%20in%20Korea.pdf

Mont, O., Palgan, Y.V., Bradley, K. and Zvolska, L. (2020) A decade of the sharing economy: concepts, users, business and governance perspectives, *Journal of Cleaner Production*, 269: 122215.

Mullen, C.A. (2021) Why mobility justice means prioritising accessible walking environments. Active Travel Studies, 1(1), DOI: 10.16997/ats.1066

Murphy, L., Samanani, F., Button, M., Emden, J., Stone, L. and Mackintosh, D. (2021) *London: A Just Transition City*, London: Institute for Public Policy Research.

Nab, C. and Maslin, M. (2020) Life cycle assessment synthesis of the carbon footprint of Arabica coffee: case study of Brazil and Vietnam conventional and sustainable coffee production and export to the United Kingdom, *Geo: Geography and Environment*, 7: e00096.

Colorado Energy Office (2023) 2023 Colorado EV plan [online], Available from: https://energyoffice.colorado.gov/transportation/ev-education-resources/2023-colorado-ev-plan

NationalWorld (2021) The cheapest new cars on sale in 2021 [online], Available from: https://www.nationalworld.com/lifestyle/cars/the-cheapest-new-cars-on-sale-in-the-uk-in-2021-3309470

Natural England (2019) *Monitor of Engagement with the Natural Environment: The National Survey on People and the Natural Environment* [online], Available from: https://assets.publishing.service.gov.uk/media/5d6cd601e5274a170c435365/Monitor_Engagement_Natural_Environment_2018_2019_v2.pdf

Nimrod, G. (2014) The benefits of and constraints to participation in seniors' online communities, *Leisure Studies*, 33: 247–66.

Norwegian Ministry of Climate and Environment (2022) *Norway's Climate Action Plan for 2021–2030* [online], Available from: https://www.iea.org/policies/14454-climate-action-plan-20212030

Oakman, J., Kinsman, N., Stuckey, R., Graham, M. and Weale, V. (2020) A rapid review of mental and physical health effects of working at home: how do we optimise health? *BMC Public Health*, 20: 1825.

O'Connell, R., Owen, C., Padley, M., Simon, A. and Brannen, J. (2019) Which types of family are at risk of food poverty in the UK? A relative deprivation approach, *Social Policy and Society*, 18: 1–18.

OECD (2022) *A Framework to Decarbonise the Economy* (OECD Economic Policy Papers No. 31), DOI: 10.1787/4e4d973d-en

OECD (2023) *Climate Action Monitor* [online], Available from: https://www.oecd.org/en/publications/the-climate-action-monitor-2023_60e338a2-en.html

Office for National Statistics (2018) *Regional Economic Activity by Gross Value Added (balanced)*, Newport: Office for National Statistics.

Office for National Statistics (2019a) *Exploring the UK's Digital Divide*, Newport: Office for National Statistics.

Office for National Statistics (2019b) *Household Debt in Great Britain: April 2016 to March 2018*, Newport: Office for National Statistics.

Office for National Statistics (2019c) *Household Total Wealth in Great Britain: April 2018 to March 2020*, Newport: Office for National Statistics.

Office for National Statistics (2020) *Labour Market in the Regions of the UK*, Newport: Office for National Statistics.

Office for National Statistics (2025) *Living Costs and Food Survey* [online], Available from: https://www.ons.gov.uk/surveys/informationforhouseholdsandindividuals/householdandindividualsurveys/livingcostsandfoodsurvey#:~:text=The%20Living%20Costs%20and%20Food,basket%20of%20goods%20and%20services

Ofqual (2021) *Summer 2021 Student-Level Equalities Analysis*, Coventry: Office of Qualifications and Examinations Regulation.

International Olympic Committee (2023) The IOC's climate commitment [online], Available from: https://www.olympics.com/ioc/sustainability/climate

Oreskes, N. (2004) The scientific consensus on climate change, *Science*, 306: 1686.

Oswald, Y., Owen, A. and Steinberger, J.K. (2020) Large inequality in international and intranational energy footprints between income groups and across consumption categories, *Nature Energy*, 5: 231–9.

Overman, H.G. and Xu, X. (2024) Spatial disparities across labour markets, *Oxford Open Economics*, 3: i585–610.

Owen, A. and Barrett, J. (2020) Reducing inequality resulting from UK low-carbon policy, Climate Policy, 20: 1193–208.

Owen, A. and Kilian, L. (2020) *Consumption-based Greenhouse Gas Emissions for Bristol 2016*, University of Leeds [online], Available from: https://www.bristolonecity.com/wp-content/uploads/2020/05/Consumption-based-Greenhouse-Gas-Emissions-for-Bristol.pdf

Owen, A., Middlemiss, L., Brown, D., Davis, M., Hall, S., Bookbinder, R., Brisbois, M.C., Cairns, I., Hannon, M. and Mininni, G. (2023) Who applies for energy grants? *Energy Research & Social Science*, 101: 103123.

Pagán, R. (2015) The contribution of holiday trips to life satisfaction: the case of people with disabilities, *Current Issues in Tourism*, 18: 524–38.

Palomo-Domínguez, I., Elías-Zambrano, R. and Álvarez-Rodríguez, V. (2023) Gen Z's motivations towards sustainable fashion and eco-friendly brand attributes: the case of Vinted, *Sustainability*, 15: 8753.

Papargyropoulou, E., Lozano, R., Steinberger, J., Wright, N. and Ujang, Z.B. (2014) The food waste hierarchy as a framework for the management of food surplus and food waste, *Journal of Cleaner Production*, 76: 106–15.

Paramio Salcines, J.L., Grady, J. and Downs, P. (2014) Growing the football game: the increasing economic and social relevance of older fans and those with disabilities in the European football industry, *Soccer and Society*, 15: 864–82.

Paterson, M., Wilshire, S. and Tobin, P. (2024) The rise of anti-net zero populism in the UK: comparing rhetorical strategies for climate policy dismantling, *Journal of Comparative Policy Analysis: Research and Practice*, 26: 332–50.

Pemberton, S.A. (2015) *Harmful societies: understanding social harm*, Bristol: Policy Press.

Pennington, R. (2018) Social media as third spaces? Exploring Muslim identity and connection in Tumblr, *International Community Gazette*, 80, 620–36.

Perlaviciute, G., Steg, L. and Sovacool, B.K. (2021) A perspective on the human dimensions of a transition to net-zero energy systems, *Energy and Climate Change*, 2: 100042.

Perreault, T. (2020) Bolivia's high stakes lithium gamble: the renewable energy transition must ensure social justice across the supply chain, from solar panels and electric vehicles to the lithium extraction that fuels them, *NACLA Report on the Americas*, 52: 165–72.

Pfeffer, F.T. (2008) Persistent inequality in educational attainment and its institutional context, European Sociological Review, 24(5): 543–65.

Picco, P. (2008) Multicultural libraries' services and social integration: the case of public libraries in Montreal Canada, *Public Library Quarterly*, 27: 41–56.

Poruschi, L. and Ambrey, C.L. (2018) Densification, what does it mean for fuel poverty and energy justice? An empirical analysis, *Energy Policy*, 117: 208–17.

Powells, G. and Fell, M.J. (2019) Flexibility capital and flexibility justice in smart energy systems, *Energy Research & Social Science*, 54: 56–9.

Quilley, S. (2013) De-growth is not a liberal agenda: relocalisation and the limits to low energy cosmopolitanism, *Environmental Values*, 22: 261–85.

Reames, T.G. (2016) Targeting energy justice: exploring spatial, racial/ethnic and socioeconomic disparities in urban residential heating energy efficiency, *Energy Policy*, 97: 549–58.

Renel, W. (2019) Sonic accessibility: increasing social equity through the inclusive design of sound in museums and heritage sites, *Curator: The Museum Journal*, 62: 377–402.

Reynolds, C.J., Horgan, G.W., Whybrow, S. and Macdiarmid, J.I. (2019) Healthy and sustainable diets that meet greenhouse gas emission reduction targets and are affordable for different income groups in the UK, *Public Health Nutrition*, 22: 1503–17.

Rhubart, D., Sun, Y., Pendergrast, C. and Monnat, S. (2022) Sociospatial disparities in 'third place' availability in the United States, *Socius: Sociological Research for a Dynamic World*, 8: 237802312210903.

Rice, P.G. and Venables, A.J. (2021) The persistent consequences of adverse shocks: how the 1970s shaped UK regional inequality, *Oxford Review of Economic Policy*, 37: 132–51.

Rinne, A. (2018) The dark side of the sharing economy [online], Available from: https://www.weforum.org/agenda/2018/01/the-dark-side-of-the-sharing-economy/

Robins, N. (2020) *Policy Brief: Financing a Just Transition to Net-Zero Emissions in the UK Housing Sector*, Grantham Research Institute on Climate Change and the Environment [online], Available from: https://www.lse.ac.uk/granthaminstitute/wp-content/uploads/2020/07/Financing-a-just-transition-to-net-zero-emissions-in-the-UK-housing-sector.pdf

Robinson, M. and Shine, T. (2018) Achieving a climate justice pathway to 1.5°C, *Nature Climate Change*, 8: 564–9.

Rosemberg, A. (2010) Building a just transition: the linkages between climate change and employment, International Journal of Labour Research, 2(2, Climate Change and Labour: The Need for a 'Just Transition'): 124–62.

Roser-Renouf, C., Maibach, E.W., Leiserowitz, A. and Zhao, X. (2014) The genesis of climate change activism: from key beliefs to political action, *Climate Change*, 125: 163–78.

Ross, A., Van Alstine, J., Cotton, M. and Middlemiss, L. (2021) Deliberative democracy and environmental justice: evaluating the role of citizens' juries in urban climate governance, *Local Environment*, 26: 1512–31.

Royce, E. (2018) *Poverty and Power: The Problem of Structural Inequality*, Lanham, Maryland: Rowman & Littlefield.

Saatcioglu, B. and Corus, C. (2014) Poverty and intersectionality: a multidimensional look into the lives of the impoverished, *Journal of Macromarketing*, 34, 122–32.

Sahay, T. (2024) Liberal blindspots, *Phenomenal World* [online], Available from: https://www.phenomenalworld.org/analysis/liberal-blindspots/

Sarlio-Lähteenkorva, S. and Lahelma, E. (2001) Food insecurity is associated with past and present economic disadvantage and body mass index, *Journal of Nutrition*, 131: 2880–4.

Sasse, T., Allan, S. and Rutter, J. (2021) *Public Engagement and Net Zero: How Government Should Involve Citizens in Climate Policy Making*, London: Institute for Government.

Savage, T., Akroyd, J., Mosbach, S., Hillman, M., Sielker, F. and Kraft, M. (2022) Universal digital twin – the impact of heat pumps on social inequality, *Advances in Applied Energy*, 5, DOI: 10.1016/j.adapen.2021.100079

Scheer, R. (2023) Virtual tourism: Better for the planet than actual tourism? [online], Available from: https://emagazine.com/virtual-tourism/

Schor, J.B. (2017) Does the sharing economy increase inequality within the eighty percent? findings from a qualitative study of platform providers. *Cambridge Journal of Regions, Economy and Society*, 10: 263–79.

Schor, J.B. and Fitzmaurice, C.J. (2015) Collaborating and connecting: the emergence of the sharing economy, in: L. Reisch and J. Thogersen (eds) *Handbook of Research on Sustainable Consumption*, Cheltenham: Edward Elgar, p 410.

Schor, J.B., Fitzmaurice, C., Carfagna, L.B., Attwood-Charles, W. and Poteat, E.D. (2016) Paradoxes of openness and distinction in the sharing economy, *Poetics*, 54: 66–81.

Scott, C., Sutherland, J. and Taylor, A. (2018) *Affordability of the UK's Eatwell Guide*, London: The Food Foundation.

Scott, D. and Gössling, S. (2021) Destination net-zero: what does the international energy agency roadmap mean for tourism?, *Journal of Sustainable Tourism*, 30(1): 14–31.

Scott, M. and Powells, G. (2020) Towards a new social science research agenda for hydrogen transitions: social practices, energy justice, and place attachment, *Energy Research & Social Science*, 61: 101346.

Scott, R. (2011) The role of public libraries in community building, *Public Library Quarterly*, 30: 191–227.

Shannon, J. (2016) Beyond the supermarket solution: linking food deserts, neighborhood context, and everyday mobility, *Annals of the American Association of Geographers*, 106: 186–202.

Sheller, M. (2020) Mobility justice, in M. Büscher, M. Freudendal-Pedersen, S. Kesselring, and N. Grauslund Kristensen (eds) *Handbook of Research Methods and Applications for Mobilities*, Cheltenham: Edward Elgar, p 11.

Sheller, M. and Urry, J. (2016) Mobilizing the new mobilities paradigm, *Applied Mobilities*, 1: 10–25.

Shove, E. and Walker, G. (2014) What is energy for? Social practice and energy demand, *Theory, Culture & Society*, 31: 41–58.

Silveira, A. and Pritchard, P. (2016) *Justice in the Transition to a Low Carbon Economy* (Working Paper No. 04/2016), Cambridge: University of Cambridge Institute for Sustainability Leadership (CISL).

Simcock, N., Jenkins, K.E.H., Lacey-Barnacle, M., Martiskainen, M., Mattioli, G. and Hopkins, D. (2021) Identifying double energy vulnerability: a systematic and narrative review of groups at-risk of energy and transport poverty in the global north, *Energy Research & Social Science*, 82: 102351.

Skeggs, B. (1997) *Formations of Class and Gender*, London: Sage.

Slater, S., Baker, P. and Lawrence, M. (2022) An analysis of the transformative potential of major food system report recommendations, *Global Food Security*, 32: 100610.

Snell, C. (2022) Global climate justice in N. Yeates and C. Holden (eds) *Understanding Global Social Policy* (3rd edn), Bristol: Policy Press.

Snell, C., Bevan, M. and Thomson, H. (2015) Justice, fuel poverty and disabled people in England, *Energy Research & Social Science*, 10: 123–32.

Snell, C., Lambie-Mumford, H. and Thomson, H. (2018a) Is there evidence of households making a heat or eat trade off in the UK? Journal of Poverty and Social Justice, 26: 225–43.

Snell, C., Anderson, S. and Thomson, H. (2023) If not now, then when? Pathways to embed climate change within social policy, *Social Policy & Society*, 22: 675–94.

Snell, C., Pleace, N., Browning, A. and Anderson, S. (2024) *Fuel Poverty and Homelessness: Exploring the Extreme End of the Cost of Living Crisis*, York: University of York.

Snell, C., Bevan, M., Gillard, R., Wade, J. and Greer, K. (2018b) *Policy Pathways to Justice in Energy Efficiency* [online], Available from: https://eprints.whiterose.ac.uk/139942/

Snell, C.J., Scott, M., Jenkins, K., Kennedy, K., Thomson, H., Yenneti, K., Stockton, H. and Gough, I. (2022) Climate justice, social policy, and the transition to Net Zero, *Social Policy Review 34: Analysis and Debate in Social Policy 2022*, 24: 5–23.

Sovacool, B.K. and Dworkin, M. (2014) *Global Energy Justice: Problems, Principles and Practices*, Cambridge: Cambridge University Press.

Sovacool, B.K., Furszyfer Del Rio, D.D. and Griffiths, S. (2021) Policy mixes for more sustainable smart home technologies, *Environmental Research Letters*, 16: 054073.

Sovacool, B.K., Kester, J., Noel, L. and de Rubens, G.Z. (2019) Energy injustice and Nordic electric mobility: inequality, elitism, and externalities in the electrification of Vehicle-to-Grid (V2G) transport, *Ecological Economics*, 157: 205–17.

Stantcheva, S. (2022) Inequalities in the pandemic, *Economic Policy* [online], Available from: https://scholar.harvard.edu/files/stantcheva/files/inequalities_pandemic.pdf

Steinberger, J.K., Krausmann, F. and Eisenmenger, N. (2010) Global patterns of materials use: a socioeconomic and geophysical analysis, *Ecological Economics*, 69: 1148–58.

Stephenson, M.L. and Hughes, H.L. (2005) Racialised boundaries in tourism and travel: a case study of the UK black Caribbean community, *Leisure Studies*, 24(2): 137–60.

Stern, N.H. (2007) *The Economics of Climate Change: the Stern Review*, Cambridge: Cambridge University Press.

Streimikiene, D., Lekavičius, V., Baležentis, T., Kyriakopoulos, G.L. and Abrhám, J. (2020) Climate change mitigation policies targeting households and addressing energy poverty in European Union, *Energies*, 13: 3389.

Sudmant, A., Robins, N. and Gouldson, A. (2021) Tracking local employment in the green economy: the PCAN Just Transition Jobs Tracker, *Place-Based Climate Action Network* [online], Available from: https://pcancities.org.uk/tracking-local-employment-green-economy-pcan-just-transition-jobs-tracker

Suresh, A. (2023) *Identifying Low Carbon Sources of Man-made Cellulosic Fibres (MMCF)*, UNFCCC [online], Available from: https://unfccc.int/documents/630806

Taheraly, L., Ghamkhar, R. and Talaty, U. (2023) *Identifying Low Carbon Sources of Sheep Wool, Hair, Alpaca Fiber and Silk Fiber*, UNFCCC [online], Available from: https://unfccc.int/documents/630805

Tauschinski, J., Sogomonian, T. and Boelman, V. (2019) Flipping the Coin: the Two Sides of Community Wealth in England, London: The Young Foundation.

Taylor Aiken, G., Middlemiss, L., Sallu, S. and Hauxwell-Baldwin, R. (2017) Researching climate change and community in neoliberal contexts: an emerging critical approach, *Wiley Interdisciplinary Reviews: Climate Change*, 8: e463.

Taylor, M., White, K.M., Caughey, L., Nutter, A. and Primus, A. (2023) Unique and cheap or damaged and dirty? Young women's attitudes and image perceptions about purchasing second hand clothing, *Sustainability*, 15: 16470.

The Federal Government (2020) *Building and Housing* [online], Available from: https://www.bundesregierung.de/breg-en/issues/climate-action/building-and-housing-1795860

The Food Foundation (2021) *The Broken Plate: The State of the Nation's Food System* [online], Available from: https://foodfoundation.org.uk/sites/default/files/2021-10/FF-Broken-Plate-2021.pdf

The Health Foundation (2024) *Inequalities in Access to Green Space* [online], Available from: https://www.health.org.uk/evidence-hub/our-surroundings/green-space/inequalities-in-access-to-green-space#:~:text=green%20space%20deprivation).-,People%20who%20live%20in%20more%20deprived%20areas%20are%20more%20likely,in%20the%20least%20deprived%20neighbourhoods

REFERENCES

The Young Foundation (2019) *Flipping the Coin: The Two Sides of Community Wealth in England* [online], Available from: https://i3w7d2w8.stackpathcdn.com/wp-content/uploads/2019/11/Flipping-the-Coin-Report-2019.pdf

Thew, H., Middlemiss, L. and Paavola, J. (2020) 'Youth is not a political position'? Recognition and representation justice in the UNFCCC, *Global Environmental Change*, 61, DOI: 10.1016/j.gloenvcha.2020.102036

Tingay, R.S., Tan, C.J., Tan, N.C.W., Tang, S., Teoh, P.F., Wong, R. and Gulliford, M.C. (2003) Food insecurity and low income in an English inner city, *Journal of Public Health*, 25(2), 156–9.

Tobi, R., Driscoll, M. and Gurung, I. (2023) *Low Income, Low Emissions? A Briefing Exploring Whether Reducing the Emissions Footprint of UK Diets is Equally Achievable for Different Income Groups* [online], Available from: https://foodfoundation.org.uk/sites/default/files/2023-07/TFF_CLIMATE%20BRIEFING.pdf

Törnberg, P. (2022) How sharing is the 'sharing economy'? Evidence from 97 Airbnb markets, *PLOS ONE*, 17: e0266998.

Transport for the North (2023) Transport-related social exclusion in England, ArcGIS StoryMaps [online], Available from: https://storymapsdev.arcgis.com/portal/apps/storymaps/stories/f9763ffd85544332b84fc48aa0e9b0b4.

Turman, W., Doucet, B. and Diwan, F. (2021) Living through a pandemic in the shadows of gentrification and displacement: experiences of marginalized residents in Waterloo Region, Canada, in: B. Doucet, R. van Melik and P. Filion (eds) *Global Reflections on COVID-19 and Urban Inequalities, Volume 2: Housing and Home*, Bristol: Bristol University Press.

UK Government (2022) *Mission Zero: Independent Review of Net Zero*, Gov.uk [online], Available from: https://assets.publishing.service.gov.uk/media/63c0299ee90e0771c128965b/mission-zero-independent-review.pdf

UK Government (2024) Help from your energy supplier: the Energy Company Obligation, Gov.uk [online], Available from: https://www.gov.uk/energy-company-obligation

UN (2024a) *Secretary-General's Special Address on Climate Action: 'A Moment of Truth'* [online], Available from: https://www.un.org/sg/en/content/sg/statement/2024-06-05/secretary-generals-special-address-climate-action-moment-of-truth-delivered

UN (2024b) *Causes and Effects of Climate Change* [online], Available from: https://www.un.org/en/climatechange/science/causes-effects-climate-change

UNEP (2024) *Loss and Damage* [online], Available from: https://www.unep.org/topics/climate-action/loss-and-damage

UNFCCC (2018) Considerations Regarding Vulnerable Groups, Communities and Ecosystems in the Context of The National Adaptation Plans [online], Available from: https://unfccc.int/sites/default/files/resource/Considerations%20regarding%20vulnerable.pdf

UNFCCC (2020a) *Just Transition of the Workforce, and the Creation of Decent Work and Quality Jobs* [online], Available from: https://unfccc.int/sites/default/files/resource/Just%20transition.pdf

UNFCCC (2020b) *Sweden's Long Term Strategy for Reducing Greenhouse Gases*, [online], Available from: https://unfccc.int/sites/default/files/resource/LTS1_Sweden.pdf

UNFCCC (2023) *What is the United Nations Framework Convention on Climate Change?* [online], Available from: https://unfccc.int/process-and-meetings/what-is-the-united-nations-framework-convention-on-climate-change

UNISON (2024) Closure of more than a thousand youth centres could have lasting impact on society: teenagers left isolated and without advice or safe spaces. [online], Available from: https://www.unison.org.uk/news/2024/06/closure-of-more-than-a-thousand-youth-centres-could-have-lasting-impact-on-society/

UNRISD (2018) *Mapping Just Transition(s) to a Low-Carbon World*, Just Transition Research Collaborative [online], Available from: https://www.uncclearn.org/wp-content/uploads/library/report-jtrc-2018.pdf

Unsworth, K.L. and Fielding, K.S. (2014) It's political: how the salience of one's political identity changes climate change beliefs and policy support, *Global Environmental Change*, 27: 131–7.

Vakinn (2024) *Certified Companies* [online], Available from: https://www.vakinn.is/en/certified-companies

Valor, C., Ronda, L. and Abril, C. (2022) Understanding the expansion of circular markets: building relational legitimacy to overcome the stigma of second-hand clothing, *Sustainable Production and Consumption*, 30: 77–88.

Verlinghieri, E. and Schwanen, T. (2020) Transport and mobility justice: evolving discussions, *Journal of Transport Geography*, 87: 102798.

Visit Iceland (2024) *Sustainability Certifications and Projects in Iceland* [online], Available from: https://www.visiticeland.com/article/sustainability-certifications-and-projects-i-iceland

von Platten, J., Mangold, M. and Mjörnell, K. (2020) Energy inequality as a risk in socio-technical energy transitions: the Swedish case of individual metering and billing of energy for heating, *IOP Conference Series: Earth and Environmental Science*, 588: 032015.

Vona, F., Marin, G., Consoli, D. and Popp, D. (2015) Green Skills. Working Paper Series, National Bureau of Economic Research [online], Available from: https://www.nber.org/system/files/working_papers/w21116/w21116.pdf

Walker, G. and Day, R. (2012) Fuel poverty as injustice: integrating distribution, recognition and procedure in the struggle for affordable warmth, *Energy Policy*, 49: 69–75.

Walker, G., Mitchell, G. and Pearce, J. (2017) Pollution and inequality, in A.R.H. Dalton (ed) *Annual Report of the Chief Medical Officer 2017: Health Impacts of All Pollution – What Do We Know?* [online], Available from: https://www.gov.uk/government/publications/chief-medical-officer-annual-report-2017-health-impacts-of-all-pollution-what-do-we-know

Wang, X. and Lo, K. (2021) Just transition: a conceptual review, *Energy Research & Social Science*, 82: 102291.

Wästerfors, D. and Hansson, K. (2017) Taking ownership of gaming and disability, *Journal of Youth Studies*, 20: 1143–60.

Watson, P., Morgan, M. and Hemmington, N. (2008) Online communities and the sharing of extraordinary restaurant experiences, *Journal of Foodservice*, 19: 289–302.

Webb, J., Qureshi, A., Frost, S. and Massey-Chase, B. (2022) *Net Zero Places: A Community-Powered Response to the Climate Crisis*, IPPR North [online], Available from: https://www.ippr.org/articles/net-zero-places

White, R. (2013) *Environmental Harm: An Eco-Justice Perspective*, Bristol: Policy Press.

Williams, R.D. (2018) Boundaries, third spaces and public libraries, in: G. Chowdhury, J. McLeod, V. Gillet and P. Willett (eds) *Transforming Digital Worlds*, Cham: Springer International Publishing, pp 703–12.

World Meteorological Association (2018) WMO Statement on the State of the Global Climate in 2019, Geneva: WMO.

WRAP (2024) *The Courtauld Commitment 2030* [online], Available from: https://www.wrap.ngo/taking-action/food-drink/initiatives/courtauld-commitment

Xie, Y., Fang, M. and Shauman, K. (2015) STEM education, *Annual Review of Sociology*, 41: 331–57.

Yang, C., Stevens, C., Dunn, W., Morrison, E. and Harries, R. (2021) *'Why Don't They Ask Us?' The Role of Communities in Levelling Up*, London: Institute for Community Studies.

Yeates, N. and Holden, C. (eds) (2022) *Understanding Global Social Policy* (3rd edn), Bristol: Policy Press.

Young Foundation (2024) *Our Journey to Net Zero* [online], Available from: https://www.youngfoundation.org/our-work/publications/our-journey-to-net-zero/

Zero Waste Europe (2020) *France's Law for Fighting Food Waste: Food Waste Prevention Legislation* [online], Available from: https://zerowasteeurope.eu/wp-content/uploads/2020/11/zwe_11_2020_factsheet_france_en.pdf

Zimmermann, K. and Graziano, P. (2020) Mapping different worlds of eco-welfare states, *Sustainability*, 12: 1819.

Index

References to figures and photographs appear in *italic* type; those in **bold** type refer to tables.

A

accountability, distributed 105
Adams, S. 46
adaptation policy approaches 4
age related issues 47
agriculture **16**, **21**, **28**
air travel 29, 30, **31**, 59, 79
'anti-Net Zero' populist response 10
automotive industry 21
aviation tax 29, 30

B

banned products **21**, 32, 62, 63
  see also ICE (internal combustion engine) vehicles
Barrett, J. **26**
battery manufacture and disposal 50
benefit cuts 61
Bosch, G. 66
Bristol Social Exclusion Matrix (B-SEM) 17, 73–4, 75, 76
  and participation 77, 78–9, 80, 88
  and quality of life 77, 82, 84, 85, 86, 88, 98, 102
  see also exclusion, social; inclusion, social
broadband infrastructure 25, 45, 69
Brundtland Report 14

C

California **23**, **36**, 50
Calver, P. 44
Calver, P. and Simcock, N. 45, 46
Canada 8, **26**
car ownership 46, 47–8, 50–2, 59
car sharing 25
carbon allowances, personal 30
carbon capture programmes **31**
carbon emissions 15–16
  and food 7, **21**, 27, **28**, 53, *54*, 55
  and inequality 41, 79
  and consumption 61, *62*, 63
  and food 53, *54*
  and leisure 56, *57*
  and penalties for high carbon use 22, **31**, 51, 62, 63
  and policies and agreements 4, 5, 22, **31**
  carbon footprints 12–13, **21**, 27, **31**, 42, 55
  carbon tax 29, 30, **31**, 32, 48, 51, 62, 63
care system 76
carers 79, 89, 95
Centre for Research in Social Policy 61
Centre for Research into Energy Demand Solutions (CREDS) 5, 20, 25
change, affordability of **99**, 103
change, behavioural 26–7, 28, 29, 45, 54–5, 96
change, social/societal 19, 20–1, 72, 87
childcare provision 94
children 47B, 49
Chile **33**
choice, consumer 29
choice, personal 9–10, 30, 54, 86
Citizen's Assembly 26
Climate Assembly UK 5, 20, 25
climate change 2, 4, 15–16, 27, 82–3, 91
  climate change mitigation policies 1, 2, 3, 4–5, 7, 8, 70
  see also carbon emissions
Climate Change Committee (CCC) 5, 20, 107
  and everyday life 26, 29–30, 35
  and inequality 68, 69
climate crisis 1, 15–16
climate emergency 4
climate futures 19–38
  just climate futures 8–14, 85–7, 91–110
  key steps to **99**, 100–4
  see also exclusion, social; inclusion, social; inequality; justice, social
Climate Plan, Norway **31**
coffee 34
cohesion, societal/community 3, 79, 90, 110

INDEX

Colorado **26**
communities
  and inequality 44, 57–8, 62, 77
  and just climate futures 94, **99**, 100–1, 102–4, 109, 110
  and Net Zero policy change 3, 8, 106–7, 109, 110
  and social exclusion 81, 86, 90, 96, 97
communities, isolated 96, **99**
communities, wealthy 44
community action/activism 81, 107
community spaces *see* public spaces
community-based approaches 43, 44, 46, 110
conflict **16**
construction sector 67
consumption 11, **21**, 31, 32–4
  and banned products 62, 63
  and carbon emissions/carbon footprints 12, *13*, 61, *62*, 63
  and cost of living 34, 60–1
  and disabled people 62, 63, 83
  and extension of life for products 32, 33, 63
  and goods and services 12, 61, 63
  and government subsidies 32, 62
  and household income 12, *13*, 62, 63, 65
  and incentives for low carbon use 32, 33, 62
  and inequality **40**, 60–5
  and just climate futures **99**, 100
  and middle-classes 62, 64
  and production standards 32, 33
  and recycling 32, **33**
  and repair of products 32, **33**, 64
  and retrofitting of homes 60, 62
  and second-hand products 32, 64
  and sharing economy 62, 63–5
  and single-use plastics **33**, 63
  and taxation 32, 64–5
  and United Kingdom 32–3, 61
Cook, J. 15
COP24 7
Corporate Social Responsibility initiatives 28
cost of living
  and consumption 34, 60–1
  and social exclusion 89, 90, 93, 94, 97
  and social inclusion 8, 108
Courtauld Commitment 2030 **28**
COVID -19 Response and Recovery package, New Zealand **36**
COVID-19 pandemic, effects of 35, **36**, 69, 79, 109
crime 79, 82, 85
culture 79
curriculum 80
cycling 24, 49, 52, 71
  see also travel, active

D

dairy products 27, 55
debt 61, 75, 94, 95, 100
decentralization 81
  and energy 22, 44, 70–1
decision-making 49, 102–4, 110
  and social exclusion 81, 86, 90, 95, 97
DEFRA 3
deindustrialization 65, 80
demand side reduction 44–6
Department for Business, Energy and Industrial Strategy (BEIS) 5, 20
deprivation and deprived areas 12–13, 41–2, 46–7, 57, 89, 101, 102
devolution 105, 106
differences, social and historical 10, 21, 46
differences, structural 93–5
disabled people
  and inequality 47, 49, 56, 58, 62, 63, 83
  and quality of life 82, 83
  and social exclusion 82, 83
disadvantaged people 7, 12
  and inequality 48, 56, 62, 76
  and social inclusion 102, 103
disasters **16**
disease **16**, 83
disenfranchisement 95, 96, 97
diversification, lack of 67
Domestic Energy Performance Certificates (EPCs) 22, **23**
Doran, A. 49, 52

E

EAT-Lancet Commission 55
Eco-Label Certification System (ECS), Korea **33**
economic output 75
eco-social policy 14, 87
education/training opportunities 108–9
  and employment opportunities 34, 66–7, 68
  and inequality 65, 66–7, 68, 76, 80
  and social exclusion 76, 89, 90, 95, 96, 97
  and social inclusion 94, 102, 109
elderly people 101
'Eleanor' 37
electric vehicles (EVs) 6, 49–52
  and everyday life 24, 25, **26**, 37, 70
  and social exclusion 89, 90
  and social inclusion 108, 110
electricity use 6, 21, 22, 45
elitist issues 44, 51, 77
emergencies, long 105
emissions trading **31**
employment opportunities 11, **21**, 25, 34–6, 37, 84
  and carbon-intensive industries 3, 34, 67, 68, 80

and Climate Change Committee
(CCC) 35, 69
and COVID-19 35, 69
and education/training opportunities 34,
66–7, 68
and flexible working 35, 36
and green jobs 3, 9, 34, 35–6, 67–8, 69,
94, 95
and inequality **40**, 65–9, 75, 80
and just climate futures 94, **99**, 100,
101, 102
and social exclusion 69, 75, 80, 89, 90,
95, 97
and social inclusion 94, 108–9
and social justice 9, 68
and travel/transport 37, 97
and United Kingdom **35**, 65
England 67, 68, 80
and United States **36**, 66
and working from home 25, 35, 69, 80, 97
employment rates 65, 75
Energy Company Obligation **23**
energy consumption 45, 65, 76, 83, 104
and fossil fuels **23**, 34, 51, 89
energy costs 9, 22, 75, 101
and inequality 42, 58, 59, 69
energy, decentralized 22, 44, 70–1
energy efficiency 10
and homes 6, **21**, 22, **23**, 37, 42–3, 84
energy exporters 21
energy, renewable 22, **23**, **28**, 31, **36**
England
and employment opportunities 67, 68, 80
and inequality 42, 61, 67, 80
Northern England 67, 76, 89
South-East England 61, 76
Southern England 80
entertainment 58, 60
see also leisure
environmentalism 81
equal opportunities 99, 102
eudaimonia 84
European Union **26**, **31**, 75
EV charging infrastructure 6, 50, 51
everyday life 3, 10–12, 19, *20*, 72, 110
and behavioural change 26–7, 28, 29
and energy efficiency **21**, 22, **23**, 36, 37
and goods and services 24, 26
and government regulations **21**, 25, 32, **33**
and homes **21**, 22–4, 70
and incentives for low carbon use 22, **26**,
32, 33, 37
and inequality 37–8, 69–70, 74
and labelling of eco-friendly
products 28, 33
and local government policy 22, **23**, 25
and localization 30, 77
and social exclusion 74, 93

and social justice 9, 36–8, 41
and social/societal change 19, 20–1, 93
see also consumption; employment
opportunities; food; homes; leisure;
travel/transport
exclusion, social 3, 17, 73–85
and climate futures 85–7, 95–7, 101, 105
and communities 81, 86, 90, 96, 97
and cost of living 89, 90, 93, 94, 97
and debt 75, 95
and decision-making 81, 86, 90, 95, 97
and disenfranchisement 95, 96, 97
and education/training opportunities 76,
89, 90, 95, 96, 97
and employment opportunities 69, 75, 80,
89, 90, 95, 97
and everyday life 74, 93
and homes 84, 95
and rented property 95, 103
and retrofitting of homes 78, 89, 95,
97, 103
and inequality 48, 72–3, 74, 75, 86, 93
regional inequality 75, 76, 83
and left behind people 88, 92
and leisure 79, 82, 89, 96
and low-income households 75, 78, 86, 92,
93, 95, 97
and minority/disadvantaged groups 79, 82,
83, 95
and participation 78–9, 81–2, 88, 90,
96, 97
and public services 75–6, 89, 96
and quality of life 82–5, 86–7, 88
and resources, access to 74–7, 87, 88
and resources, social 74, 76–7
and social life 89, 90
and travel/transport 48, 97
and active travel 79, 82
and carers/family relationships 79, 89, 90
and electric vehicles (EVs) 89, 90
and public transport 75, 96, 101
and United Kingdom 74, 76
extension of life for products 32, 33, 63

F

family relationships 76, 79, 90
Fankhauser, S. 67
Fell, M.J. 64
flexibility 45, 78, 93, 95, 96
flexible working 35, 36
food 6–7, 11, **16**, 27–9, 44, **99**
and behavioural change 28, 29, 54–5
and carbon emissions 7, **21**, 27, **28**, 53,
54, 55
and carbon footprints **13**, **21**, 27, 55
and dairy products 27, 55
and inequality **40**, 53–6, 62, 70
and low-income households 53, 55

INDEX

and plant-based diets 6, 55
and quality of life 70, 82
and red meat 27, 54, 55
and supermarkets **28**, 28
and United Kingdom 27, **28**, 53, 54
food miles 27
food preparation/cooking **21**, 44, 55
food prices 54, 55, 62
food security **16**, 53
food supplies/supply chains 26, 27, **28**, 54
food waste 6–7, **21**, 27, 28, 54, 55–6
fossil fuels **23**, 34, 51, 89
France 28, **28**, **31**
fuel/energy poverty 59, 101
and inequality 14, 41, 42, 55, 70
and quality of life 82, 83
see also energy costs

G

G20 55
gaming industry 59
'Garot Law', France **28**
Garvey, A. and Taylor, P. 35
gas boilers 70
gender issues 46, 47, 49, 64, 65, 95, 101
gentrification 50, 52
Germany 8, 21, **23**, 25
Global North 5, 20–1, 53, 66, 98
Global South 50
goods and services
and consumption 12, 61, 63
and travel/transport 24, 26, 47, 48
governance, regional 106
government policy 109–10
local government policy 22, **23**, 25, 105, 106
national government policy 105, 106, 108
see also individual countries
grants and loans, eligibility for 43
green space 29–30, **31**, 111n3
and inequality 56–7, 59, 60
and social exclusion 79, 82, 96
Guterres, Antonio 4

H

Hargreaves, T. and Middlemiss, L. 76
harm, avoiding 85
health **16**
and inequality 14, 83–4
and quality of life 82, 83–4, 85–6, 88
Health Foundation 57
heat networks 6, **21**, 22
heating systems 9, 70, 82
and heat pumps 6, **21**, 22, **23**, 44
and hydrogen gas **21**, **23**, **35**
and smart technologies 9, 22
Henderson, J. 50
high-income households 51, 58, 59, 61, 79

holistic approach 73, 103
homes 6, 11, 22–4
and carbon footprints 12, *13*
and community-based approaches 43, 44
and energy 104
and electricity use 6, 21, 22, 45
and energy costs 42, 58, 59, 69
and energy efficiency 6, 10, **21**, 22, **23**, 37, 42–3, 84
and fuel/energy poverty 41, 42
and household income 12, *13*, 41
and inequality 10, 14, 37, 40–6, 54, 58, 59, 60, 69
and just climate futures **99**, 104
and new housing 6, 22, **23**
and older housing 6, 42, 43
and rented property **23**, 42
and smart technologies 9, **21**, 22, 44–6
and social exclusion 78, 84, 89, 95, 97
see also heating systems; retrofitting of homes
homes, location of 12, *13*
Hoole, C. 12
household occupancy/co-housing 22
human crisis 14–16
hydrogen gas 6, **21**, **23**, **35**, 44

I

ICE (internal combustion engine) vehicles 6
and everyday life **21**, 24, 25, **26**, 37
and inequality 50, 51, 62, 70
and 'Jim' 37, 89
Iceland **31**
identity, social 81
imports 32–3
incentives for low carbon use 22, 37, 103
and consumption 32, 33, 62
and travel/transport **26**, 51
inclusion, social 2, 3–4
and B-SEM 73–4, 88
and climate futures, just 10, 92, 94, 97–8, 103
and cost of living 8, 108
and education/training opportunities 94, 102, 109
and electric vehicles (EVs) 108, 110
and employment opportunities 94, 108–9
and 'leaving no one behind' policy 8, 85, 88, 97–8
and low-income households **99**, 106, 108
and minority/disadvantaged groups 98, **99**, 102, 103
and people-centred approach 85, 103, 105, 106
and retrofitting of homes 103, 108
and social life **99**, 102, 109
and technologies, new/smart 103, 108

141

income, household
  and carbon footprints 12, *13*
  and climate futures, just 94, 100, 101, 110
  and consumption 12, *13*, 61, 62, 63, 65
  disposable income
    and inequality 61, 75, 90
    and 'Jim' 90, 110
    and just climate futures 94, 100, 101, 110
    and food 53, 55
  and homes 12, *13*, 41
  and inequality 12–13, 41, 65
    and consumption 61, 62, 63, 65
    disposable income 61, 75, 90
    and food 53, 55
    and high-income households 51, 58, 59, 61
    and leisure 56, 58, 59
    and travel/transport 47, 48, *48*, 50–1
  and leisure 12, *13*, 56, 58, 59
  and social exclusion 75, 78, 86, 92, 93, 95, 97
  and social inclusion **99**, 106, 108
  and travel/transport 11, 12, *13*, 47, 48, 50–1, 79
Index of Multiple Deprivation 100
'Index of Readiness for Net Zero', Young Foundation 107
industrial revolution 15
industries, carbon-intensive
  and employment opportunities 3, 34, 67, 68, 80
  and travel/transport 21, 50
inequality 3, 7, 13, 39–71
  and behavioural change 45, 54–5
  and carbon emissions 41, 79
    and consumption 61, *62*, 63
    and food 53, *54*
    and leisure 56, *57*
  and communities 44, 57–8, 62, 77
  and consumption **40**, 60–5
  and debt 61, 75
  and deprivation and deprived areas 41–2, 46–7, 57
  and education/training opportunities 65, 66–7, 68, 76, 80
  and employment opportunities **40**, 65–9, 75, 80
  and everyday life 37–8, 69–70, 74
  and food **40**, 53–6, 62, 70
  and gender issues 46, 47, 49, 64, 65
  and Global North 53, 66
  and goods and services 12, 47, 48, 61, 63
  and health 14, 83–4
  and homes 10, 14, 37, 40–6, 54, 58, 59, 60, 69
    and community-based approaches 43, 44
    and energy costs 42, 58, 59, 69
    and energy efficiency 10, 37, 42–3

  and fuel/energy poverty 14, 41, 42, 55, 70
  and rented property 42, 43
  and retrofitting of homes 42–3, 60, 62
  and household income 12–13, 41, 65
    and consumption 61, 62, 63, 65
    disposable income 61, 75, 90
    and food 53, 55
    and high-income households 51, 58, 59, 61
    and leisure 56, 58, 59
    and travel/transport 47, 48, *48*, 50–1
  and institutional relationships 76, 77
  and IT literacy/skills 44–5, 58, 64
  and just climate futures 98, **99**, 102, 104, 105
  and kinetic elites and underclasses 49–50, 51
  and left behind people 10, 44–5, 63, 66
  and leisure/public spaces 56–8, 59, 60
  and libraries 57, 64
  and minority/disadvantaged groups
    and consumption 62, 63, 83
    and leisure 56, 57, 58, 59
    and travel/transport 47, 49
  and participation 77–9, 87
  and quality of life 83, 86–7
  and rural areas 48, 58, 64, 77
  and sharing economy 62, 63–5
  and smart technologies 14, 44–6
  and social change 72, 87
  and social exclusion 48, 72–3, 74, 86, 93
    and employment opportunities 75, 80
    regional inequality 75, 76, 83
  and social justice 39, **40**, 68, 70, 87
  and social networks 43, 77
  and spending power 61, **62**, 66
  and travel/transport 46–52, 53–4, 64
    and ICE (internal combustion engine) vehicles 50, 51, 62, 70
    and private transport **40**, 46, 47–8, 50–2, 54, 59, 62, 70
    and public transport 48–9, 52, 75
  and United Kingdom 12, 53, 65, 67, 74, 76
    and England 42, 61, 67, 80
inequality, regional 67, 68, 75, 76, 80, 83
insulation of buildings **23**, 43, 82
Intergovernmental Panel on Climate Change (IPCC), UN 4, 5, 15
IPPR (Institute for Public Policy Research) 67
IT literacy/skills 44–5, 58, 64

J

'Jim' 37, 88–90, 92, 107–10
jobs, decent 68
Jobs for Nature programme, New Zealand **36**
jobs, green 3, 9, 34, 35–6, 67–8, 69, 94, 95
Johnson, C. 46

INDEX

joined up thinking 104
JRF 61
'Just transition declaration', COP24 7
just transition initiatives 8
justice, social 7–8, 10, 17
  and everyday life 9, 36–8, 41
  and inequality 39, **40**, 68, 70, 87
  and quality of life 85, 87
  see also climate futures; exclusion, social; inclusion, social; inequality

K

Kelly, J.A. 42
kinetic elites and underclasses 49–50, 51
Korea **33**
Kyoto Protocol, UN 4

L

labelling of eco-friendly products 28, 33
LARiverWay **31**
'leaving no one behind' policy 8, 85, 88, 97–8
left behind people 10, 37, 44–5, 63, 66, 88, 92
leisure 11, **21**, 29–31, 56–9, 84
  and carbon emissions 56, *57*
  and carbon footprints 12, *13*
  and carbon tax 29, 30, **31**
  and entertainment 58, 60
  and household income 12, *13*, 58, 59
  and inequality **40**, 56–9, 60, 70, 79
  and just climate futures **99**, 109
  and minority/disadvantaged groups 57, 59, 79
  and public spaces 29–30, **31**, 56–8, 59, 60, 111n3
  and racial/ethnic issues 57, 59, 79
  and social exclusion 79, 89
  and tourism 59, 60
  and travel/transport 29, 30, **31**, 58, 59
leisure spaces *see* green space; public spaces; third spaces; virtual space
Levitas, R. 73, 85
LGBTQ+ groups 49
libraries 57, 64, 94
life, quality of 70, 82–7, 88
  and B-SEM 77, 82, 84, 85, 86, 88, 98, 102
  and just climate futures 98, **99**, 102, 103
LILI project 84
Limiting the Generation of Disposable Products and Regulating Plastics legislation, Chile **33**
lived experience 19, 40, 93
  see also employment opportunities; everyday life; food; homes; inequality; leisure; travel/transport
Living Cost and Food Survey 100, 101
living environment 84

local authorities 12, 75–6, 98
local institutions 12
'Local Law 97', New York **23**
localism 25
localization 30, 77
loneliness/isolation 69, 83
Los Angeles **31**, 36
loss and damage 4
low carbon economy 4–5, 68
low-income households
  and inequality 75
    and consumption 62, 63, 65
    and food 53, 55
    and leisure 56, 59
    and travel/transport 47, 48, 50–1
    and social exclusion 75, 78, 86, 92, 93, 95, 97
    and social inclusion **99**, 106, 108
Lubitow, A. 48–9
Lucas, K. 47
Lucas, K. and Pangbourne, K. 52
luxury products 34

M

manufacturing industry 65–6, 67, 80
marginalization 81, 85, 102
Marmot Review Team 83
Massachusetts Community Climate Bank **23**
meat, red 27, 54, 55
mental health problems 69, 82, 83
middle-classes 37, 62, 64, 81
migration **16**
minority/disadvantaged groups
  and inequality 56, 57, 58, 59
  and consumption 62, 63, 83
  and travel/transport 47, 49
  and leisure 56, 57, 58, 59, 79
  and quality of life 82, 83
  and social exclusion 79, 82, 83, 95
  and social inclusion 98, **99**, 102, 103
mobility *see* travel/transport
monitoring progress of Net Zero policy 107
mortality rates 83
Mullen, C.A. 52
multinational organizations 28–9

N

National Food Strategy 55
Nationally Determined Contributions (NDCs) 5
natural resources 50
Neighbourhood A, Leeds 40–1, 61, 65, 108
Neighbourhood A, Newcastle 53, 60
Neighbourhood B, Leeds 108
Neighbourhood B, Newcastle 56
Neighbourhood C, Leeds 46–7
Neighbourhood C, Newcastle 109–10
Nestle **28**

'Net Zero', life under 5–7
  see also everyday life; inequality
Net Zero policy and planning 1–5, 7–10, 13–14, 19–38, 99–110
  see also everyday life; exclusion, social; inclusion, social; inequality; justice, social
Netherlands 68
New York 23
New Zealand 36
North America 26
Norway 21, **31**
'nudging' 28

O

OECD countries 65
older people 45, 58, 61, 82
Oreskes, N. 15
Owen, A. and Barrett, J. 101

P

Paris Agreement 4, 5, 7
Paris Olympics **31**
participation
  and B-SEM 77, 78–9, 80, 88
  and inequality 77–9, 87
  and just climate futures 95, 98, 102, 103, 107, 109–10
  and social exclusion 78–9, 81–2, 88, 90, 96, 97
participation, economic 78
participation, political 81–2, 95, 97, 102, 109–10
participation, social 78–9, 109
pedestrians 52
penalties for high carbon use 22, **31**, 51, 62, 63
people-centred approach 85, 103, 105, 106
place 8–9, 11–12, 77
place-based approach 105, 106–7
Place-based Climate Action Network (PCAN) 36
plant-based diets 6, 55
plastics, single-use **33**, 63
pollution 52, 82, 83
poverty see low-income households
Powells, G. and Fell, M.J. 45
power, corporate 29
power, distribution of 12
production standards 32, 33
public health 82–3
public services 75–6, 89, 96, 100, 104–5
public spaces
  and everyday life 29–30, **31**, 111n3
  and inequality 56–8, 59, 60
  and social exclusion 79, 82, 89, 96

R

racial/ethnic issues 47, 49, 57, 59, 79, 95
Rare Earth Element (REE) mining 50

raw materials, use of 32
Reames, T.G. 43
recycling 32, **33**, 109
refrigerators 32
regulations, government **21**, 25, 32, **33**
relationships, institutional 76, 77
rented property **23**, 42, 43, 95, 103
repair of products 32, **33**, 64
resources, access to 74–7, 87, 88
resources, social 74, 76–7
retraining see education/training opportunities
retrofitting of homes 22, 70
  and consumption 60, 62
  and inequality 42–3, 60, 62
  insulation of buildings **23**, 43, 82
  and social exclusion 78, 89, 95, 97, 103
  and social inclusion 103, 108
  see also heating systems
right-wing politics 10
Risk Assessment, CCC 107
risk aversion 78
road building 25
Robins, N. 46
Rosemberg, A. 66
rural areas 11, 48, 58, 64, 77, 96

S

safety issues 48–9, 52
Sahay, T. 10
Scotland 8
Scott, M. and Powells, G. 44
second-hand products 32, 51, 64
sector-specific policies 35
sharing economy 62, 63–5
Shaw, Chris 10, 91
shopping, online 27
siloed thinking 103, 104
Silveira, A. and Pritchard, P. 68
Snell, C. 43
social life 47, 89, 90, 92, **99**, 102, 109
social media 58, 109
social networks 43, 77, 94, 100
social policy 14
  see also exclusion, social; inclusion, social; justice, social
social relations 76–7
solar panel installation 37
Sovacool, B.K. 51
Spain 8
spending power 13
  and flexibility 78, 93, 95, 96
  and inequality 61, **62**, 66
spending, public 75–6, 105
stamp duty 22
subsidies, government see incentives for low carbon use
suburban areas 13, 48
Sudmant, A. 67

supermarkets 28
supply chains 27, **28**, 34, 54, 67
Sweden **26**, **35**

T

taxation 22, 48, 51, 62, 63
  and consumption 32, 64–5
  and leisure 29, 30, **31**
technologies, new/smart 96
  and homes 9, **21**, 22, 44–6
  and inequality 14, 44–6
  and social inclusion 103, 108
third spaces 57–8
Tobi, R. 55
tourism **31**, 59, 60
training *see* education/training opportunities
trains, diesel **26**, 70–1
transformation, social 2–3, 5, 72, **99**, 103
transition pathways **99**, 103
translocality 3
transport, community 25
transport infrastructure 6, 8, 50, 59
transport, private **40**, 47–8, 50–2, 54, 59
  see also electric vehicles (EVs); ICE (internal combustion engine) vehicles
transport, public 6, 24–5, 94
  and inequality 48–9, 52, 75
  and social exclusion 75, 96, 101
Transport Related Social Exclusion tool 100
travel, active 6, 24–5, **26**, 30, **31**, 71
  and inequality 48, 49, 50, 52
  and social exclusion 79, 82
travel/transport 6, 9, **21**, 24–7, 35, 37, 70
  and air travel 29, 30, **31**, 59
  and carbon footprints 12, *13*
  and carbon-intensive industries 21, 50
  and children 47, 49
  and employment opportunities 37, 97
  and gender issues 47, 49
  and gentrification 50, 52
  and goods and services 24, 26, 47, 48
  and government subsidies **26**, 51
  and household income 11, 12, *13*, 47, 48, 50–1, 79
  and incentives for low carbon use **26**, 51
  and inequality 46–52, 53–4, 59, 64
    and active travel 48, 49, 50, 52
    and private transport **40**, 46, 47–8, 50–2, 54, 59, 62, 70
    and public transport 48–9, 52, 75
  and just climate futures **99**, 100, 101
  and leisure 29, 30, **31**, 58, 59
  and minority/disadvantaged groups 47, 49
  and rural areas 11, 48
  and safety issues 48–9, 52
  and social exclusion 48, 97
  and active travel 79, 82
  and carers/family relationships 79, 89, 90
  and public transport 75, 96, 101
  and social inclusion 108, 110
  and taxation 29, 30
  and United Kingdom 24, **26**
  see also electric vehicles (EVs); ICE (internal combustion engine) vehicles
tree canopy **31**
trust 109–10

U

UK Census 101
'Understanding family and community vulnerabilities in transition to Net Zero' project, Nuffield Foundation 17
unemployed people **35**, 95, **99**, 101
UNFCCC 34, 68–9
United Kingdom 2, 3, 8, 12, **23**, 104–5
  and consumption 32–3, 61
  and employment opportunities **35**, 65
    England 67, 68, 80
  and food 27, **28**, 53, 54
  and inequality 12, 53, 65, 67, 74, 76
    and England 42, 61, 67, 80
  and social exclusion 74, 76
  and travel/transport 24, **26**
United Nations (UN) 4, 7–8
United States **23**, **26**, **31**, **36**, 66
upskilling/reskilling *see* education/training opportunities
urban areas 57–8, 77, 96

V

VAT (Value Added Tax) 22
ventilation of buildings 82
Victorian housing 42
virtual space 58
von Platten, J. 42–3

W

wages, average 61, 65
walking/walking routes *see* travel, active
waste collection/reduction 32, 63
water supplies **16**, **28**
welfare, sustainable 87
wellbeing 82, 83
  see also health; life, quality of
working conditions 68
working from home 25, 35, 69, 80, 97
working-class futures 10

Y

Young Foundation 77, 100, 107
young people 64, 76

www.ingramcontent.com/pod-product-compliance
Lightning Source LLC
Chambersburg PA
CBHW071713020426
42333CB00017B/2247